GLASS

A GUIDE TO CZECH & SLOVAK GLASS

Diane E. Foulds

EUROPEAN COMMUNITY IMPORTS

A GUIDE TO CZECH
& SLOVAK GLASS
Second Edition
Copyright © 1993, 1995 by Diane E. Foulds
All rights reserved.
Printed In Prague
by Libertas, a. s.

ISBN # 80-900029-6-X

Cover illustration:
"Diplomate" goblets by *Moser Co., Ltd.*
Photographer: Miroslav Vojtěchovský.

Edited by Cara M. Morris.
Book design by Miloslav Fulín.

Manufactured in the Czech Republic.

<
Vases designed by Jan Gabrhel at
Český Křišťál in Chlum u Třeboně,
1959. Photographers: Jindřich Brok
and Karel Kalivoda.

ACKNOWLEDGMENTS
I am greatly indebted to the
many individuals who
contributed their time and
knowledge to the preparation
of this book. Special thanks go
to Evelyn Bečvaříková, Olga
Drahotová, Kateřina
Lokvencová, Zdeněk Lhotský,
František Frídl, Jaroslav
Veselý, Jiří Šuhájek, Petr
Novotný, Antonín Langhamer,
Karel Leibl, Karel Holešovský,
Ladislav Jindra, Eva Ranšová,
Vladimír Horpeniak, Sylva
Petrová, Helena Brožková,
Jana Horneková, Darina Myšáková,
Oldřich Palata, Jan Mergl,
and Duňa Panenková. Above all,
I wish to express my sincere
gratitude to everyone at the
glassworks in the Czech and
Slovak Republics who so
generously provided me with
information; without their
assistance the book would not
have been possible.

INTRODUCTION

"Lasie" drinking set by the *Glass Atelier Morava* company in Vizovice, 1991. Photographer: Pavel Kosek.

WHEN the Communist system collapsed in Czechoslovakia during the last two months of 1989, the country threw open its doors to the West. Millions rushed in. They marveled at the medieval and Baroque architecture, tasted the world-famous beer, and flooded the glass shops, often buying up as much as they could carry. Some came with pushcarts and went from store to store stacking box upon box.

Why the obsession with glass? Because it is the most exciting local collectible. There were relatively few glass shops in 1989, but today there is hardly a street in Prague's inner city without at least one display window shimmering with luxury crystal.

The Czechs and Slovaks are not the only glass producers in Central Europe, but they have few rivals in terms of range and artistry. The art of glassmaking goes back 600 years in Bohemia, and this illustrious tradition is clearly evident in the high level of craftsmanship. What is truly remarkable is that even though most of the crystal is made by hand, it can still be bought at prices well below what you'd pay in London, Paris, Milan, or New York for glass of comparable quality.

Now that the state-run glass factories are undergoing privatization, they are increasingly free to make their own decisions about the kind of glass they produce and how and to whom they sell it.

Likewise, Western importers are no longer forced to go through state channels - although, because details about these factories are scarce, some of them still do.

This guide is an attempt to fill the gap by providing practical, up-to-date information on producers and retail outlets, and on the glass industry as a whole. As the first complete resource book of its kind, it aims to supply visitors to the Czech Republic and Slovakia with all the background knowledge they need to make an informed decision about what to purchase during their stay. The book is also intended to aid those dealing with glass on a commercial level.

Every effort has been made to ensure complete and accurate information. However, the ongoing decentralization and privatization of the economy in both Czech and Slovak Republics can only mean that company names, addresses, and telephone numbers will continue to change from day to day. Rather than wait out this process, I have opted to describe the state of the glass industry as it is today, and to add updates to future editions. Please address any questions or comments to: European Community Imports, Ltd., Šlikova 40, CZ – 169 00 Prague 6, Czech Republic. Information has been obtained from reliable sources, but to err is only human. The correctness of the data presented here is not guaranteed.

Table of contents

<
Vase designed by Petr Hora,
made at the *Beránek Glassworks* in
Škrdlovice. Photographer: Miroslav
Vojtěchovský.

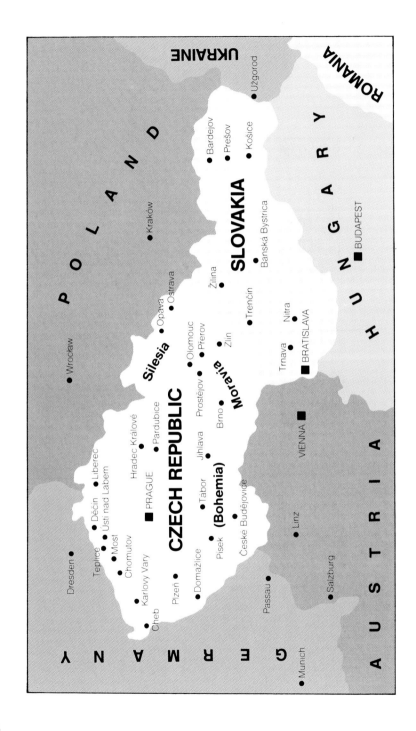

PART I • THE BASICS

A sandpit in
Hrdoňovice,
near Jičín.
Photo: ČTK.

WHAT IS GLASS?

GLASS is essentially a mixture of sand and metal oxides melted down at extremely high temperatures to a thick, glue-like substance which is then shaped and cooled. About 70% of the mixture is sand (silica). The Venetian glassmakers used the fine sand of the Po River, while those in Bohemia obtained their sand from ground-up quartz. The exact recipe determines the hardness, brilliance, and color of the glass, and is often kept a professional secret. In ancient times, glass was valued as a substitute for precious gems or for rock crystal, a popular engraving material but one difficult to find in its pure form.

Most glass belongs to one of three types: soda-lime, potash-lime, or potash-lead. The ingredients for potash-lime, the most common type in Bohemia, formerly came from leaching, or filtering, the ashes of beech trees with

11

water. This "forest glass," or "Bohemian glass" as it is sometimes called, was refined over the centuries. The need for wood as a basic component of glass explains why early glassmakers settled in remote areas of the countryside - the forests provided abundant raw materials for the glass base, as well as sufficient fuel to heat the stone and clay furnaces. As the trees were used up, the glassmakers moved on to new woodlands, sometimes leaving ghost towns behind. Even today many Czech and Slovak glassworks are in forested regions, although beech ash has been replaced by chemicals, and wood fuel by natural gas or electricity.

The Venetians, whose soda-lime glass required leaching the ashes of marine plants, produced a thin glass that was far easier to melt and manipulate, and which didn't harden as fast as Bohemian glass. Efforts to imitate this popular type of glass were never completely successful in Bohemia, but the glassmakers' experimentation led to important improvements in their own production.

A major catalyst in the development of the glassmaking industry in the Czech lands and Slovakia was the abundance of available sand. Much of it is drawn from a large pit in Střeleč near the town of Jičín in northern Bohemia. It undergoes a variety of cleansing processes to rid it of unwanted impurities, such as iron. If left in the mixture, iron particles will lend the glass a greenish cast. Ancient glassmakers didn't remove the iron, which is why bottles found in archeological digs often look green. Perfectly pure glass is not necessary for windowpanes and mirrors, so the iron is not completely sifted out. If you look closely at the edge of a mirror or at sheet glass stacked on its side, you will notice the green tint.

GLASS VERSUS CRYSTAL

YOU MAY HEAR it said about a goblet that it is "only glass - not really crystal." There is, in fact, a difference between glass and crystal, but it varies from country to country.

To most of the Western world, "crystal" signifies the presence of lead. Under European Union regulations, glassware containing less than 4% lead oxide is defined as "glass," that with a lead content greater than 10% is "crystal," and if the content is 30% or over, the designation is "high lead crystal." Most of the crystal made by the Waterford company in Ireland has a lead content of about 32%, and France's Baccarat crystal has about 34%. In the United States, glass must contain at least one percent lead to qualify as crystal. To the Czechs and Slovaks however, it is more a question of semantics. The term "crystal" can be applied to any refined, high-quality glass. Lead crystal is understood as having at least 24% lead.

The use of the word "crystal" probably stems from the days when ancient craftsmen quarried crystallized quartz (rock crystal) and made vessels out of it. The word itself is derived from the Greek *krystallos*, or "clear ice." Since pure rock crystal was rare, traders were constantly in search of a substitute, and glass posed the best solution. The 15th-century Venetians used the term to describe anything resembling rock crystal, regardless of its actual composition.

However, the English discovered refract light, so that rays shining through it will splinter into the colors of the rainbow. Crystal-gazers prefer a high lead content - 30% and over - in their crystal balls for the sake of greater depth and a broader play of light.

Although it contains no lead, *Moser* glassware is referred to as crystal because of its clarity and hardness. Photo: "Napoleon" set, *Moser Co., Ltd.*

in the 18th century that the addition of lead oxide to glass batch resulted in a striking difference in terms of sparkle and clarity.

The products of the world-famous *Moser* company in the Czech Republic are lead-free, but are regarded nonetheless as crystal because of the complex chemical makeup, clarity, and overall high quality of the glass. One of its hallmarks is its remarkable hardness. In contrast, lead content tends to soften glass, making it more amenable to cutting and engraving. Lead also adds weight to glass and makes it

The glass used to make figurines has a lead content of up to 49% to allow for maximum malleability.

A variation on crystal is crystalline. This is what Czechs and Slovaks refer to as crystal containing less than the standard 24% lead, but with a larger percent of barium oxide to provide the desired refractive qualities.

The distinction between glass and crystal is indeed apparent to the eye - you see it, for example, when a crystal chandelier flashes color spectrums around the room. The higher the lead content, the greater the brilliance. A really well-cut vase with a high lead content looks like a faceted diamond. But don't be fooled into thinking that only lead crystal is top-notch; some of the world's most elegant and expensive glass contains no lead at all.

Blowing and shaping molten glass at the *Český Křišťál* works in Chlum u Třeboně. Photographer: Lumír Rott.

IS LEAD CONTENT DANGEROUS?

IN FEBRUARY 1991, two American physicians working at New York's Columbia University published a report warning that wine kept for long periods in crystal containers could absorb dangerous levels of lead. They had tested crystal decanters containing 24-32% lead oxide, and found that tiny traces of lead began migrating into the wine within a matter of hours. Alcoholic beverages stored in many (but not all) crystal decanters for five years or longer absorbed up to 20,000 micrograms of lead per liter, instead of the 30 to 200 micrograms that wine naturally contains.

The report made headlines in the United States, and the major crystal manufacturers took action. They formed committees to conduct tests of their own. Steuben pulled its decanters off the market, and Waterford stopped selling its crystal baby bottles. To be on the safe side, the U.S. Food and Drug

Administration (FDA) issued guidelines advising consumers not to store foods in crystal containers for lengthy periods, or indeed to use crystal on a daily basis. Children and pregnant women were advised to avoid its use altogether.

Research continues, but there is still no definitive answer as to whether lead crystal really poses a health risk. The FDA was expected to issue limits by 1994 on the amount of lead allowed in crystal imported into the United States, but still has not done so.

Many crystal producers, including Czech and Slovak ones, have been advising customers for years not to leave alcoholic beverages standing for too long in crystal decanters. Alcohol can cloud fine crystal, and all alcoholic beverages evaporate over time if not stored in an air-tight container.

Unless you drink a very large amount of alcohol that has been standing for years in crystal containers, you probably need not be concerned about lead migration. A far greater risk occurs at the factory when lead crystal is melted. While the crystal is in its molten state, the lead evaporates into the air and can be inhaled by workers. Most crystal factories conduct routine blood tests on their employees to be sure their lead intake is within prescribed limits. Factories also face the problem of where to dispose of lead wastes.

If you are concerned about lead, stick to crystal that has a lower lead content. Most Czech and Slovak glass is lead-free. Cut glass identified as lead crystal usually contains 24%, although some types contain 10%. Certain styles at *Český Křišťál* in Chlum u Třeboně are in this category. To test lead migration yourself, write to *Frandon Enterprises*, P.O. Box 300321, Seattle, WA 98103, USA, for a Frandon Alert Kit (approx. US $ 24). Within the United States, phone (800) 359-9000 (toll-free).

HOW GLASSWARE IS PRODUCED

WATCHING glassblowers at work is a sensuous experience. A muted roar issues from the furnaces in the background. The molten glass radiates heat with a brightness that stings the eyes. The glassmakers, open-shirted and sweating, dip their long blowpipes into the furnace opening (also called the port or the glory hole), and draw out red-hot globules as soft as vaseline. They work harmoniously, skillfully, purposefully, with supreme economy of movement. There is little conversation. Making a piece of glass is an act of teamwork, with each worker dependent on the others. Timing and precision are essential, because glass cools quickly.

This is an almost exclusively male domain - women do not blow glass in Central Europe, owing, in part, to the physical nature of glassblowing, the strength required to hold up heavy masses, or gathers, of glass, and the hot, sweaty conditions. But there is also a ritual involved here, and traditions die hard.

In earlier times, the production hall was a highly patriarchal environment with a strict pecking order. To a certain extent that hierarchy has endured. In a traditional glassworks, each glory hole is attended by a team of three to four workers whose tasks are strictly defined. There is the master or gaffer, who is the most skilled and experienced of the group, the chief blower, and two helpers who fetch the glass from

molten state 24 hours a day, which means that the production hall is a warm place. A furnace may have three to eight glory holes from which the glassblower, using a 5-foot long iron blow-pipe, lifts out the required quantity.

A craftsman cutting pre-sketched designs into a lead crystal bowl at the *Harrachov* glassworks. Photo: ČTK.

the furnace and hand the master the necessary tools. The master is usually easy to distinguish: he is the one seated.

Glass in the raw looks something like flour tossed with brown sugar. Unmelted lead crystal resembles chili powder - the lead oxide is bright orange. *Glass Atelier Morava*, which uses only first-class imported materials, gets its raw glass in the form of round white pellets from Holland.

Once melted down to a fluorescent orange soup at temperatures of up to 1,400 degrees C (2,520 degrees F), the glass stays in its

A ball of molten glass is placed into a moistened wooden mould, the mould is closed, and the blower blows through his spinning mouthpipe until the molten glass coats the walls of the mould. The mould is then opened and the glass is lifted out in its new shape. It is frequently taken back to the heat of the furnace so as not to cool. The blowpipe is then handed to the master, who shapes the stem and foot by spinning it against a wet wooden tool held in one hand. At each step of the way the scalding glass is shaped, snipped, spun, and reheated to prevent cooling.

When it is completed, a goblet is knocked off the end of the pipe with a well-aimed blow, and an assistant carries it on the end of a long padded fork to the annealing oven, where it will sit for two to four hours until the temperature of the glass has cooled slowly enough to prevent cracking.

However efficiently the team works as a whole, mishaps do occur. The forearms of a veteran glassmaker are often covered with scars, each one testimony to the hazards of working with red-hot materials. Nearby is the crate where failed attempts are thrown. These shards of glass, called cullet, will be broken up and recycled into the next batch.

At each step in the process, there is the danger of breakage. Goblets are broken at the furnace, as they are knocked off the blowpipe, en route to the annealing oven, inside it, on their way to the cutting room, on the cutting wheel, in the storage room, and in shipment. One inopportune sneeze can mean the end of a piece that has already spent two weeks in production. A bad batch of glass can yield so many bubbles and impurities that only one in every ten goblets is worth saving. And having one glassblower out sick can throw a monkey wrench into production unless a stand-in can be found.

What goes into a goblet after it has left the annealing oven depends on its degree of decoration. The first step is to cut or burn away the excess glass at the top that was attached to the blowpipe, known as the cap or deposit. The sharp edge left over is sanded or burned down until it is smooth. The piece is then polished, cut, painted, etched, glazed, or engraved, whatever the case may be. A vase blown at *Moser* might require another two to six months of finishing before it is ready to be inspected, sorted, wrapped, and readied for shipment.

A machine-made goblet, on the other hand, can be slung out on a production line in a matter of seconds. *Crystalex, Sklo Bohemia* in Světlá nad Sázavou, and *Lednické Rovne* have lines that produce up to 60,000 pieces a day. The price difference says it all. The machine-made goblet might sell for USD $3 or $4 in a discount store, while its handmade counterpart will go for 10 to 20 times that amount at Harrod's or Bloomingdale's.

HOW TO DISTINGUISH QUALITY

A TRULY top-quality piece of glass is easy to recognize: it looks solid, it feels good in the hand, its colors have a cleanness about them, and, if uncolored, it possesses the luster of fine crystal. Although it is sometimes claimed that good glass will give off a clear ring when tapped with a spoon, in fact this resonance usually reveals more about the shape and thickness of the piece than its quality.

The flaws to watch out for are irregular swirls or layers, cords, bubbles, nicks, rashes, and rough or dull areas. These are likely indications of impure raw materials. If you are examining cut glass, look for evenness and sharpness of cut (but it shouldn't be too sharp!). Hold the piece up and inspect it from the bottom and from various angles - does the design conceal flaws or bubbles? With elaborate cuts and poor store lighting, these flaws might not show up until you're halfway home. The most challenging test for a lead crystal producer is to leave a vase undecorated. With no designs to conceal them, impurities in the glass become more readily apparent. So for lead crystal with few cuts, high-quality glass is essential.

A seam running down the length of the stem is a dead giveaway that a goblet was made by machine. If so, it will also have a slight ridge around the lower rim of the foot. The seams are even easier to see in pressed glass, which is rarely as pure and clear as the hand-blown or even the machine-made variety. Sometimes you can spot the latter from the way the bowl connects to the stem. If the joint is ever so slightly uneven, or if the stem seems to flow into the bowl, your glass is probably hand-blown. The absolutely perfect, geometrically-straight joint is the mark of automation.

SHIPPING GLASSWARE

THE BEST WAY to ship glass is to wrap it up like a Russian Matryoshka doll, putting a box inside a box inside a box, each one separated by padding. Museums that are used to shipping valuable glassware usually wrap each glass individually in tissue paper soft enough not to scratch the surface. An extra wad of tissue paper is bound around the rim. Then the item is placed inside a box filled with styrofoam "popcorn," wooden fibers, or bunched-up tissue paper, so that the glass itself at no point touches the side of the box. That box is sealed and placed in a wooden crate or sturdy outer case that can't be dented if dropped or thrown. More styrofoam or bunched newspaper is inserted between the inner and outer boxes. As a final precaution, the package is labeled "glass" in big, black letters, and insured against breakage.

What if it breaks anyway? If you packed and mailed the item yourself, you might be out of luck, unless you have insured it and can collect on the insurance. If the shop is handling the shipping for you, make sure you ask for a receipt with a written guarantee that broken pieces will be replaced.

In the event of damage, you will have to send either the piece affected or a photo of it back to the shop. Most stores pack their glass well to forestall such claims.

HOW TO CARE FOR QUALITY GLASS

AS WITH any fine collectibles, glassware must be kept clean. Protect it from dampness, sudden changes of temperature, and strong sunlight. Store it whenever possible in a dust-free environment, such as a glass case or cabinet. Dust combined with moisture can have a corrosive effect on glass, but this is easily prevented with a little regular care.

To wash glass, use very warm - not hot - water, and any kind of detergent as long as it is free of abrasives. Hand-dry immediately with a soft cotton cloth to prevent water spots. A window-washing liquid is recommended for vases, sculpture, figurines, or any glass other than table ware.

Whatever you do, don't put delicate glassware in the dishwasher! Gushes of scalding water will wear down the crystal. It might also dull gold plating, crack small filaments, and chip fine edges. If you discover a chip, try sanding it over ever so carefully with the finest grain of sandpaper, or ask an expert to do it for you. This ensures that you'll be able to drink from the glass safely.

If all else fails, before you throw a favorite piece away in despair, consult the glass specialist or restorer at your local museum. They are experts at salvaging damaged treasures.

PART TWO • THE HISTORY OF CZECH AND SLOVAK GLASSMAKING

THE ORIGINS OF GLASSMAKING

THE VERY FIRST glass objects were probably beads.

Glassmaking goes all the way back to the cradle of civilization itself, ancient Mesopotamia, on the territory of today's Iraq and Syria. Small pieces of glass as well as glass objects have been found there that date from the middle of the third millennium B.C.

The invention of the blowpipe in the first century B.C. revolutionized glassmaking. For the first time, hollow vessels such as beakers, bottles, and cups could be made quickly and in relatively large quantities.

Archeologists have excavated rings and beads in areas of Moravia and Slovakia settled by Slavic tribes in the 5th and 6th centuries. Craftsmen in Bohemia started blowing glass in the 13th and 14th centuries, primarily in monastery workshops.

Among the earliest objects produced were cups and roundels (small round discs used as windows). As local skills grew more sophisticated, colorful stained-glass windows with intricate Biblical scenes were made for churches and cathedrals. Few Gothic stained-glass windows have survived in the Czech lands. Those in the church of St. Bartholomew in Kolín, however, are well preserved, and date from about 1380. An exceptional work is the glass wall mosaic of *The Last Judgment* which presides over the south portal of St. Vitus cathedral in the Prague Castle complex. It dates from 1370, during the illustrious reign of Emperor Charles IV. Mosaics of this type and period are rare so far north of the Alps. Craftsmen from Murano were probably responsible for this striking example of the glassmaker's art.

By the late 1300s, probably more than 20 glassworks were operating in Bohemia and Moravia. Their wares consisted primarily of roundels, but also included vials, bot-

tles, cups, beakers, and mirrors. Conditions for glassmaking were particularly favorable in northern Bohemia, where all the necessary raw materials were in plentiful supply: quartz to make the glass, vast beech forests to fuel the furnaces and provide the potash, moulds, and tools. The oldest still functioning glassworks in the Czech lands is at *Chřibská* (in German Kreibitz), founded in 1414 in the hills near the border with Saxony.

Very little is known about the early history of glassmaking in Slovakia, which was part of the Kingdom of Hungary until 1918. The first recorded glassworks were established in the mid-14th century. We know that glass was blown in Bardejov by 1434, and the local museum has a number of Venetian-inspired Renaissance cups bearing the town crest. The eastern town of Košice was one of the most important glass-painting centers on Slovak territory in the fifteenth century.

In Bohemia, some 40 glassworks were in operation by the end of the 16th century, competing with foreign producers for lucrative European markets. (Oddly enough, the number of factories today is about the same, although there were as many as 79 in 1799 and 177 in 1883.) Glass tableware was a luxury item reserved for the high nobility, on whose estates the glass furnaces were built. Later it became accessible to wealthy land-

owners and merchants as well. A typical Renaissance beaker might bear a family's coat of arms ornamented in gold.

Bohemian glass producers achieved their first major international success in the mid-16th cen-

Cobalt blue glass tankard with enamel painting, northern Bohemia, *c.* 1590. Photo: Museum of Decorative Arts, Prague. Photographer: Gabriel Urbánek.

Enamel cold-painted (unfired) beakers with diamond engraving, Bohemia: *A Couple*, 1620 (left), and *The Crucifixion*, 1614 (right). Photo: Museum of Decorative Arts, Prague. Photographer: Gabriel Urbánek.

tury with the Venetian-inspired technique of colored enamel painting on drinking vessels. These were usually beakers and goblets, as well as bottles with coats of arms, human figures, and proverbs painted in white, red, yellow, green, and blue. Enamel-painted bottles with folk-art motifs are still popular today.

VENETIAN, GERMAN, AND ENGLISH INFLUENCES

TODAY there is hardly a country in Europe that doesn't have its own glass industry, but only a handful of glassmaking centers enjoy worldwide reputa-

tions. They include the island of Murano in the Venetian lagoon, Baccarat in France, Orrefors in Sweden, Waterford in Ireland - and, of course, Bohemia. All these

countries have contributed significantly to the development of glass as an art form, but the parameters of mutual influence are not so clear. As in the case of other arts, European glass is ultimately a study in cross-fertilization.

From the 16th to the mid-17th century, Venetian glass was the finest in the world. Its delicate, simple lines were unequaled. Bohemian glass was considerably thicker and heavier. The silica and potassium forest glass of Central Europe did not lend itself as easily to refined shapes and complex ornamentation. Landlocked Bohemia and Saxony had difficulty obtaining the marine plants needed to make Venetian soda glass.

Although Venetian glassmaking methods were a strictly guarded secret, eventually they spread north to Germany and from there to Bohemia and Slovakia. Many German glassmakers, particularly from Saxony, migrated east in search of work, so that by the end of the 16th century, several Bohemian glassworks were doing their best to imitate Venetian styles.

The most important glassworks were located in the primarily German-speaking areas of Bohemia, and the vast majority of the inventors, decorators, entrepreneurs, and factory owners from the 15th to the early 20th centuries were German or of German descent. The Czechs and Slovaks were more likely to work in their factories as glassblowers. Many of the glass trends Germans helped create were sold on German markets by German-speaking merchants living in Bohemia or Slovakia.

Since German and Bohemian glassmakers traveled back and forth, employed similar techniques, and catered to the same clientele, stylistically the Bohemian and German glass of the period are hard to tell apart.

In the third quarter of the 17th century, a unique chemical mixture was concocted that would become known throughout the world as Bohemian crystal. This was a new type of potash-lime glass containing a high proportion of chalk (calcium carbonate). It was clearer and more brilliant than Venetian glass, but still thick enough to engrave. By the end of the century, Venice's fragile beakers were passé and elaborately engraved Bohemian crystal was the rage in Europe. It remained the most sought-after luxury glass throughout the 18th century, and was even sold in Venice until its import was forbidden. This Baroque period was the golden era of Bohemian glass.

The Baroque art of engraving glass probably originated in ancient Rome, but it reached its height in Prague. In 1583, the Habsburg Emperor Rudolf II, a sophisticated art collector with a passion for precious gems, transferred his court from Vienna to Prague, which soon became an important gem-cutting center. The German jeweler Caspar Lehmann was appointed "Imperial Gem Engraver" in 1601; he is credited with having been the first to apply gem-engraving techniques to hollow glass. By the first half of the 18th century, Steinschönau (today Kamenický Šenov) and its environs had become the leading center of glass engraving.

Engraved Baroque cup, Bohemia, c. 1720. Photo: Museum of Decorative Arts, Prague. Photographer: Gabriel Urbánek.

25

Engraved
Barogue
goblets with
elaborate pin-
cer-formed
stems,
Bohemia, c.
1680 (left) and
c. 1720 (right).
Photo: Museum
od Decorative
Arts, Prague.
Photographér:
Gabriel
Urbánek.

Engraved wine
jug, Bohemia,
c. 1700. Photo:
Museum of the
City of Prague.
Photographers:
Zdenka
Kalabisová and
Antonín Krčmář.

Three cut goblets, Bohemia, 1690-1720. Photo: Museum of Decorative Arts, Prague. Photographer: Gabriel Urbánek.

Courtly scene painted in enamel on a Rococo beaker, Bohemia, c. 1770. Photo: Museum of Decorative Arts, Prague. Photographer: Gabriel Urbánek.

Gilded beaker with commercial motifs, Bohemia, c. 1770. Photo: Museum of Decorative Arts, Prague. Photographer: Gabriel Urbánek.

Around the same time, the earliest crystal chandeliers were being produced in Steinschönau (Kamenický Šenov). Royal clients were delighted by the novelty of lighting fixtures hung in shimmering crystal, and orders poured in from all over Europe.

New ways of coloring and decorating glass were introduced in the course of the 18th century. The fruits of this explosion in creativity included ruby glass, enamel-painted glass, gilded glass, white milk-glass imitating porcelain, and glass painted with the black filigree patterns *(Schwarzlot)* of Ignaz Preissler, who worked in both glass and porcelain. A glass factory manager and alchemist in Potsdam, Johann Kunckel, revived the ancient technique of gold-sandwich glass, in which gold decoration was enclosed between two fused layers of glass. Glassmakers in Bohemia improved on this technique by using gold leaf instead of paint.

Advances were also made in costume jewelry, with the production of glass beads that were difficult to distinguish from precious stones.

Beakers painted by Ignaz Preissler in black filigree *(Schwarzlot),* Bohemia, probably Kunštát, c. 1730. Photo: Museum of Decorative Arts, Prague. Photographer: Gabriel Urbánek.

Balustroid goblet painted with gold in the gold-sandwich technique *(Zwischengoldglas),* Bohemia, c. 1730. Photo: Museum of Decorative Arts, Prague. Photographer: Gabriel Urbánek.

Milk glass imitating porcelain, painted and gilded, from *Harrachov* in Neuwelt (Nový Svět), *c.* 1790. Photo: Museum of Decorative Arts, Prague. Photographer: Gabriel Urbánek.

Pharmaceutical glass, western Slovakia, 17th-18th centuries. Photo: Slovak Glass Museum, Lednické Rovne. Photographer: Daniel Zachar.

There were glassworks throughout Slovakia already in the 17th century, in most cases on the estates of the Hungarian nobility or the Catholic Church. Skilled Czech and German workers were invited to build new factories. Glass manufacturing was concentrated in central Slovakia. To the east, however, sheet glass was produced, as well as a variety of domestic articles, such as bottles, jugs, pitchers, jars, and a type of flask called a *kuttrolf*, which had a twisted neck to prevent liquids from flowing out more than a drop at a time.

The manufacture of utility glass increased in the 18th century. Such wares were intended for use by village residents and in taverns and roadside inns. Local decorators wove regional folk-art motifs into their designs, with the result that their work often displayed more originality than the fashionable glassware made for the nobility, which was dependent on imported styles.

Between 1711 and 1806, there were 47 glassworks in Slovakia. Some produced elegant colored and decorated vessels of cobalt blue and milk glass, in addition to the more prosaic jugs and oil-lamp cylinders.

Bohemia had established itself as a world leader in decorated glass by the 1730s. As demand steadily rose, the producers formed trading companies and opened warehouses in the major ports of Europe. Village schools in north- ern Bohemia offered instruction in half a dozen foreign languages to train local boys for careers in inter- national sales: markets ranged from New England to the bazaars of Cairo and Constantinople.

The invention of lead crystal in

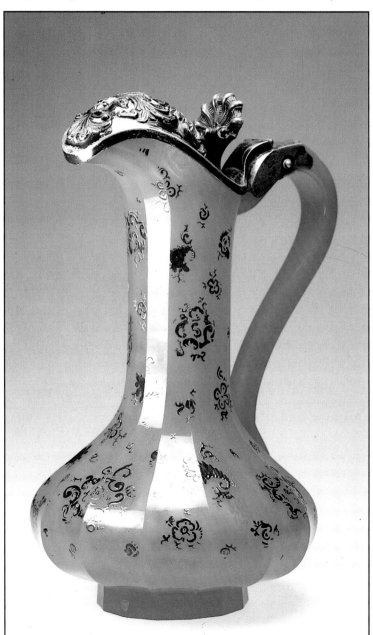

Silver-painted alabaster jug, Bohemia, c. 1840. Photo: Museum of Decorative Arts, Prague. Photographer: Gabriel Urbánek.

England ultimately helped topple Bohemian glass from its dominant position. George Ravenscroft had discovered that adding lead oxide to molten glass gave it the colorless, brilliant properties lacking in Venetian glass, and in 1674 he

Bohemia learned how to make lead crystal at lower cost, mastered the English cutting designs, and then went a step further by engraving the glass as well as cutting it. Bohemia's trade links within Europe were damaged

Cup and saucer of hyalite glass, gold *chinoiserie* painting, southern Bohemia, *c.* 1825. Photo: Museum of Decorative Arts, Prague. Photographer: Gabriel Urbánek.

applied for a patent. He perfected his formula two years later. Nevertheless, cut lead crystal had no palpable impact on the market until the end of the 18th century, when English and Irish glass cutters introduced designs that fully exploited its unprecedented clarity and brilliance. The French and the Belgians followed suit. Lead crystal would remain the most fashionable type of glass well into the next century.

To compete, glassmakers in

by the Napoleonic Wars, however, so rebuilding a strong market position required even greater resourcefulness.

By the 1830s, with the craze for colorless lead crystal fading, the time was ripe to introduce something new. The answer was colored glass, both opaque and transparent. Bohemian glassmakers excelled at creating vividly colored objects that were elaborately cut, engraved, and painted - at times to excess.

Beaker cut, gilded, and painted with transparent enamel, northern Bohemia, c. 1830. Photo: Museum of Decorative Arts, Prague. Photographer: Gabriel Urbánek.

Cased and engraved beaker with Friedrich Egermann's famous red stain, from the *Egermann* studio in Haida (Nový Bor), after 1832. Photo: Museum of Decorative Arts, Prague. Photographer: Gabriel Urbánek.

Decanter and beaker, overlay with ruby glass and white enamel, cut, painted, and gilded, from *Harrach* in Neuwelt (Nový Svět), c. 1850. Photo: Museum of Decorative Arts, Prague. Photographer: Gabriel Urbánek.

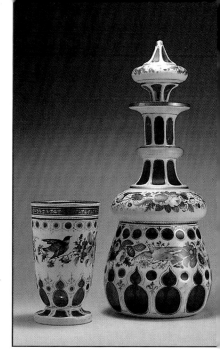

The leading producers of the Biedermeier period were the *Harrach* works in Neuwelt (Nový Svět), which still operates today in the Giant Mountains near the Polish border, and the *Buquoy* works in Gratzen (Nové Hrady), in southern Bohemia. An important figure in the development of Bohemian glass was Friedrich Egermann, a painter and inventor who experimented with different forms of decoration. Egermann invented lithyaline glass, an opaque variety that resembled basalt and red marble. His innovations also included the rediscovery of a bright yellow stain and the invention of a cranberry-colored one, which earned him considerable fame and is still produced today.

Another new technique was to apply a layer of transparent color to the glass, and then cut or engrave it away to expose the clear crystal underneath. This is known as layered, or cased, glass. Sometimes a third layer was applied, usually white enamel, and after cutting the glass was painted with gold leaf and floral motifs. The result is referred to as overlay glass.

The Bohemian glass industry drew on the skills of a virtually inexhaustible supply of local cutters and engravers. When their numbers exceeded available jobs, these artisans left Bohemia in search of work. Ultimately they contributed to the success of rival glassmaking centers abroad.

Cut and engraved crystal pitcher from
the *J. & L. Lobmeyr Co.* in
Steinschönau (Kamenický Šenov),c.
1880 photo: Museum of Decorative
Arts, Prague.
Photographer: Gabriel Urbánek.

Lithyaline glass, c. 1830. Photo:
Museum of Decorative Arts.
Photographer: Gabriel Urbánek.

Wine and sherry glasses with hot-shaped stems from *Katarínska Huta* in Slovakia, 1900-05. Photo: Slovak Glass Museum, Lednické Rovne. Photographer: Daniel Zachar.

Cased and cut carafe from *Katarínska Huta,* second half of the 19th century. Photo: Slovak Glass Museum, Lednické Rovne.. Photographer: Daniel Zachar.

Hot-shaped pitcher of rose glass, central Slovakia, second half of the 19th century. Photo: Slovak Glass Museum, Lednické Rovne. Photographer: Daniel Zachar

ALTHOUGH glass is also manufactured in neighboring Moravia, Silesia, and Slovakia, it is in Bohemia, a region about the size of Maine, that glass production has historically been concentrated. Characteristic of Bohemian glass is the sheer profusion of its styles, some original and some borrowed. As international trends came and went, Bohemian producers possessed the uncanny ability not only to reproduce the prevailing style but to improve upon it.

In the 16th century, while attempting to imitate Venetian glass, they invented a more colorless version that was also more durable. In the 18th century, they developed milk glass which looked like porcelain but was much less expensive. When the English introduced cut lead crystal, it took Bohemia's glassmakers only a short time to come up with a cheaper variety with more ornate designs. The pressure of competition from the English was felt once again with the advent of Josiah Wedgwood's black matte basaltware pottery in the 1820s. The *Buquoy* works in southern Bohemia quickly offered customers a good approximation: an opaque glass called hyalite, which was nearly identical but not as expensive. And Bohemian glassmakers took the late-19th-century Art Nouveau style - made famous by Louis Comfort Tiffany and Émile Gallé - to dazzling new heights.

If the producers in Bohemia had a weakness, it was their tendency to rest on their laurels once they were riding a wave of success. It was not uncommon for them to discover that a foreign competitor had beaten them to the invention of the latest trend. Then, to keep up with the market, they would scramble to adopt the new style, in the course of which they would discover some special feature to make it their own.

Virtually every decorating technique imaginable had been invented by the 20th century, and nearly all were in use in the Bohemian glass industry.Those that originated in Bohemia included Egermann's red stain, black hyalite (usually with gold chinoiserie decoration), marble-like lithyaline glass, the translucent alabaster glass of the pre-1848 Biedermeier period, uranium glass with its fluorescent lime-yellow hues, and ceramic inlays, which glassmakers at the *Harrach* works applied on glass.

What distinguishes Bohemian glass from that made in other parts of Europe is a solidness in its appearance that stems from the Middle Ages. Bohemian glass of the modern era has not differed greatly in style or shape from that produced elsewhere, apart from contemporary glass art. But even in the area of sculpture, where individual artistic styles are highly diverse, the overall uniqueness of Czech - and also Slovak - glass often boils down to a solid simplicity of form.

PART THREE • 20TH-CENTURY CZECH AND SLOVAK GLASSMAKING

GLASSMAKING BEFORE WORLD WAR II

THE TURN of the 20th century brought another golden age to glassmakers in Bohemia, where probably more artisans were engaged in the production of luxury crystal than anywhere else in Europe, apart from France. The Art Nouveau style, or *Jugendstil,* was flourishing in Vienna, and several members of the *Wiener Secession* artists' group produced iconoclastic designs for production in Bohemian factories.

The 1900 World Exhibition in Paris, the most prestigious glass show of the day, awarded its coveted Grand Prix to three companies specializing in Art Nouveau: Gallé in France, Tiffany in the United States, and Bohemia's *Loetz* works at Klostermühle (Klášterský Mlýn). In Prague, a Bohemian version of the *Secession* was founded in 1908 called the Artěl group, which offered its own unique interpretation of Art Nouveau in glass and other media.

Iridized Art Nouveau vase with embedded threads from the *Johann Loetz Witwe* glassworks in Klostermühle (Klášterský Mlýn), 1901. Photographer: Gabriel Urbánek.

Iridized Art Nouveau vase with hot-shaped handles from *Johann Loetz Witwe,* 1902. Photographer: Gabriel Urbánek.

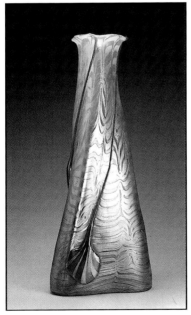

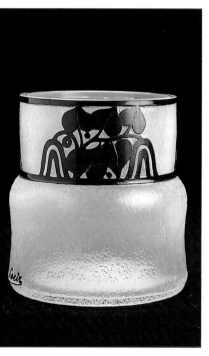

Vase of blue opal glass by Viennese designer Josef Hoffmann, *Johann Loetz Witwe*, 1911. Photo: Museum of Decorative Arts, Prague. Photographer: Gabriel Urbánek.

Overlay, etched, gilded, and black-painted vase from *Johann Loetz Witwe*, 1913. Photo: Museum of Decorative Arts, Prague. Photographer: Gabriel Urbánek.

World War I interrupted glass production, but in the independent Czechoslovak state that emerged from the ruins of the Austro-Hungarian Empire in 1918, creativity returned in full force. The new country inherited the lion's share of the industry in the former Monarchy, including 92% of its glass production. The ailing postwar economy at home forced companies to seek foreign markets for almost all their luxury glass. But find them they did. Czechoslovakia managed to carve out over 10% of the international glass market by the end of the 1920s.

"Canaan, the land of plenty": cup engraved by Jaroslav Horejc for the *J.& L. Lobmeyr Co.*, 1922. Photo: Museum of Decorative Arts, Prague. Photographer: Gabriel Urbánek.

44

Art Deco egg-shaped glass container designed by Václav Špála of the Artěl artists' group, Prague, 1924. Photo: Museum of Decorative Arts, Prague. Photographer: Gabriel Urbánek

Art Deco jar with enamel painting, designed by Josef Eiselt, Bohemia, 1924. Photo: Museum of Decorative Arts. Photographer: Gabriel Urbánek.

Cut glass vase designed by Ludvika Smrčková, the *Rückl* glassworks in Nižbor, c. 1935. Photographer: Gabriel Urbánek

Another great success for the industry was the new modern style of Art Deco, which had replaced the flowery motifs of Art Nouveau by the early 1920s. Leading Viennese artists continued to have their designs produced in factories in the Nový Bor and Kamenický Šenov region. Glass designers toyed with a variety of styles up until the 1930s, then launched full tilt into functionalism, which stressed simplicity, practicality, and usefulness. Several functionalist drinking sets designed by Ludvika Smrčková at the *Rückl* works in Nižbor won international awards.

In Slovakia, glass manufacturers began to lose their foothold on foreign markets already at the end of the 19th century. The situation in the 1920s and 1930s was even worse, with some factories either switching their production lines from artistic to technical glass or shutting down completely. A notable exception was the glassworks at *Uhrovec* in central Slovakia, where the designer Štefan Šovanka created superbly etched and overlay Art Nouveau glass inspired by the work of Émile Gallé. The modernized *Lednické Rovne* works was also successful in the twenties, producing beautifully thin-walled goblets with pantographed etchings for European luxury hotels. Perhaps the greatest challenge facing Slovakia's glass industry was competition from Bohemia, which was experiencing a boom.

A trio of training schools for glassmakers, located in the northern Bohemian towns of Kamenický Šenov, Nový Bor, and Železný Brod, became recognized centers of glass design in the inter-war period. *Moser* introduced the use of rare earth colors such as alexandrite (lilac), royalite (rose), and beryl (aqua), which were an immediate hit with foreign buyers. The 1925 International Exhibition of Decorative Arts in Paris awarded seven top honors to recipients in Bohemia: these were Jaroslav Horejc, a glass engraver and professor at the Prague Academy of Applied Arts; the glassworks of *Harrachov* in Neuwelt (Nový Svět) and *Riedel* in Polaun (Polubný), today part of Desná; all three glassmaking schools; and the Academy of Applied Arts in Prague.

The bubble burst with the onset of the Great Depression, when markets collapsed across Europe and North America and many Bohemian and Slovak producers were forced to halt production for lack of orders. The industry rebounded in the latter half of the 1930s, and by 1936, it was producing 40% of the world's glass. Czechoslovakia had become one of the 10 leading industrialized nations, with a gross domestic product larger than England's. Two years later the country was dismembered by Hitler.

THE COMMUNIST YEARS

THE 20TH CENTURY has been a turbulent period for Czechs and Slovaks. Since 1938 they have experienced the breakup of Czechoslovakia, Nazi occupation, nationalization of industry, Stalinist terror, collectivization of agriculture, Soviet invasion, political repression, and most recently - following the fall of the Communist regime in 1989 - the country's division into two independent states. In the course of these traumatic upheavals, Czechoslovakia's share of the international glass market has shrunk.

In 1938, Nazi Germany annexed the country's largely German-speaking border regions, known as the Sudetenland. The most important Bohemian glassworks were in these areas, including *Moser* in Karlsbad (Karlovy Vary), the sheet glass factory in Teplitz (Teplice), the luxury glass producers *Kreibitz* (Chřibská) and *Harrachov* (Neuwelt), the *Riedel* factories and many other producers of glass raw materials near Desná, and a vast number of costume jewelry, chandelier, and decorating studios in *Steinschönau* (Kamenický Šenov), *Haida* (Nový Bor), and *Gablonz* (Jablonec nad Nisou). These factories, now incorporated into the Third Reich, went into rapid decline after war broke out in 1939 and drained away manpower and raw materials; some works were converted to military production.

A handful of factories in the remaining part of the Czech lands, which was occupied by the Nazis in March 1939, carried on making glass, including the works in Poděbrady, Nižbor, and Železný Brod. Meanwhile, experimentation in design and technique continued in the glass department of the Academy of Applied Arts in Prague, encouraged by Karel Štipl, Josef Kaplický, and other influential teachers.

In the years following the Allied victory in 1945, the overwhelming majority of ethnic Germans, numbering over three million, were rounded up and driven out of Czechoslovakia. They included owners and managers of glass factories, technicians, designers, and decorators. Among the few Germans allowed to remain was Stefan Rath, who had inherited the prestigious *J.& L. Lobmeyr Co.* in Kamenický Šenov from his uncle, Ludwig Lobmeyr, in 1918. Although forced to relinquish ownership of the company to the state in 1948, Rath stayed on as manager until 1951, when he moved to Vienna. Other Sudeten Germans opened glassworks in Austria and Germany, which today still produce many of the same models for which they were known in prewar Bohemia.

Upon its return to power, the Czechoslovak government of Eduard Beneš issued an edict nationalizing all major industrial plants, including glassworks and large decorating workshops. The north Bohemian glass factories were in shambles; fuel and raw materials were scarce, and the glassmakers had to scavenge for sand and wood. With the Sudeten Germans gone, there were doubts as to whether the Czechs and Slovaks could summon the skills and know-how necessary to save what was left of the glass industry.

In Prague, however, a group of recent graduates of the glass department at the Academy of Applied Arts were determined to see the industry through its crisis. Stanislav Libenský, René Roubíček, Miluše Roubíčková, and Josef Hospodka were among its leading members. They and other young artists and technicians went north to the major glass-producing areas of Nový Bor, Kamenický Šenov, Teplice, and Jablonec nad Nisou, and taught glassmaking and decorating skills. They worked closely with the factories while producing their own inspired designs, some of which were on an architectural scale.

Czechoslovak exports of household glass resumed in the summer of 1945 and did relatively well until 1947, when the impact of foreign competition began to be felt. In an effort to remedy the situation, a centralized trade enterprise called *Glassexport* was set up to handle sales. In 1948, the Communists seized power in Prague and private ownership was abolished.

Following the Soviet paradigm, the country's Communist leadership placed all economic activity in the hands of central planners and began a systematic process of collectivization. Monolithic state entities were created from scores of small decorating workshops and individual factories. At first the glassworks were organized by region; later they were reorganized according to the type of glass they produced. The only producer to escape this consolidation was the small *Beránek* company in Škrdlovice, which was consigned to liquidation. Supporters waged a battle to save it, and the state finally declared it an art center under the supervision of the Ministry of Culture. Special institutions advised factories on design, in particular the Main Creative Center for the Glass and Fine Ceramics Industry, established in Prague in 1952 and renamed the Institute for the Design and Production of Furniture, Furnishings, and Apparel (ÚBOK) in 1958.

The specialized glassmaking schools in Kamenický Šenov and Nový Bor were closed, and the long-established contacts that so many glass companies had developed with foreign buyers were disrupted. Several Western nations erected punitive customs barriers against imports of Czechoslovak products to protest the Communist takeover. With orders down, state authorities gave serious consideration to terminating glass production in some factories and converting them to other types of industry.

As it was, production levels in the early 1950s dropped considerably. Glassblowers were lured into heavy industry by the promise of higher wages. Few apprentices were trained, and skills that had been passed down for generations were suddenly lost. Production was halted for good on many of the fabulously ornate perfume-bottle stoppers that had been routinely produced in the Desná area, for example; today there are no glassblowers left who know how to produce them.

The glass industry fared poorly under state control. Worker motivation was low, and productivity fell. Factory managers were selected on the criteria of political

reliability rather than experience or management skills. The government, coasting on the long-established reputation of Bohemian glass, declined to invest in expensive advertising and promotion campaigns. As a result, foreign competitors soon surged ahead in the international marketplace.

Soviet domination meant that a large percentage of the country's glass output had to be sold to Mos-

Cut and engraved lead crystal vase bearing the emblems of the Stalinist 1950s: a star, the hammer and sickle, a tractor, and a dedication to Klement Gottwald, Czechoslovakia's first Communist president. Northern Bohemia, c. 1952. Photo: Museum of Decorative Arts, Prague. Photographer: Gabriel Urbánek.

Engraved lead crystal vase from the heyday of socialist realism, northern Bohemia, c. 1957. Photo: Museum of Decorative Arts, Prague. Photographer: Gabriel Urbánek.

cow and other members of the Communist trading bloc. These markets were not nearly as lucrative or as exacting as those in the West. Czechoslovak glassmakers no longer had to compete with the world's best, and less pride went into their work. Production plans came from above, often based on weight or volume with little regard for quality. Under a five-year plan based on weight, for example, large, heavy pieces would be produced in an attempt to meet production targets, while small, delicate articles would be neglected.

Although the state built several new glass factories and modernized and renovated many older ones over the years, these efforts never seemed to keep pace with the needs of the industry. Other industrialized nations had long since incorporated modern mass-production facilities, particularly for pressed glass, by the time they were installed in Czechoslovakia in the 1960s and 1970s.

But advances were made in the industrial sphere. Czechoslovakia was one of the first countries in the 1950s to develop foam glass, and within a short space of time it had begun the production of optical, automotive, pharmaceutical, chemical, and heat-resistant glass, as well as of glass fibers, fluorescent tubes, and specialized glass for other industrial purposes. It was one of the first nations in Europe after the war to manufacture television screens. Research institutes were set up to help develop new industrial glass technology.

For all the benefits of such discoveries, perhaps the most valuable achievement in the sphere of glass to come out of the Communist era was not foreseen in

any five-year plan; rather, it reflected the natural evolution of local glassmaking traditions and the talents of a whole new generation.

THE STUDIO GLASS MOVEMENT

"Open Window" by Stanislav Libenský and Jaroslava Brychtová, 1992. Mould-melted glass, 85 x 95 cm. Photo: Gabriel Urbánek.

STUDIO GLASS, which is essentially sculpture, is a fairly recent phenomenon. The American artists Dominick Labino and Harvey Littleton were among its pioneers in the early 1960s, but it was already off to a good start, albeit behind closed doors, in postwar Czechoslovakia.

After it was nationalized and consolidated in the 1940s, the Czechoslovak glass industry took two paths. One led to automation and the intensive development of glass for industrial uses. Quantity was more important than quality, and such things as glass fibers and automotive parts took priority over stemware. The second, unofficial path focused on glass as a fine art. It was the artists who had revitalized the devastated glass industry after the war by training new glassmakers and designing glassware for production in state-run enterprises. With furnaces and glassmaking equipment readily available, small ateliers were formed within these large complexes, and the artists pursued their own work on the side.

In Eastern Europe during the Stalinist 1950s, art was expected to conform to the principles of socialist realism. This meant cheerful, optimistic, patriotic representational art whose purpose was to inspire the working class. Writers and painters who rejected the doctrine ran the risk of persecution, and abstract art was held in contempt. Glass, however, was overlooked by the cultural czars; artists working in this medium were allowed to go about their business relatively unhindered. The official thinking seems to have been that glass was a functional, ornamental medium, not an expressive one - how can you make a political statement in the design of a goblet? Not a few painters and graphic artists took refuge in studio glass as a way of escaping harassment and retaining a modicum of creative freedom. Under the umbrella of the large state-run glass enterprises, artistic experimentation thrived. Artists like Stanislav Libenský, Josef Kaplický, and their pupils managed to break new ground without bowing to pressure from above. Their achievements furthered Czechoslovakia's reputation abroad as a leader in glass design and, not incidentally, earned the country badly needed hard currency. For the artists, working for the state had its advantages, not the least of which was a steady income.

During the early fifties, the country was hermetically sealed off from the West. All but the best-known artists were forbidden to travel outside the Soviet bloc. For that reason, teachers exercised a strong influence on the direction glass art took. Josef Kaplický, then head of the glass department at Prague's Academy of Applied Arts, was intent on keeping up with Western trends. He also insisted that his students study a variety of media - drawing, ceramics, painting, sculpture - and apply them to glass. Stanislav Libenský, who succeeded Kaplický in 1963, continued this approach. Generations of young Czech artists came of age under these two masters, and an atmosphere of tolerance and creativity prevailed.

For years the West hardly suspected that such exciting experimentation was going on behind the Iron Curtain. Its first exposure internationally came in 1957, at the International Exhibition of Decorative Arts in Milan, and a year later at the World's Fair in Brussels. Visitors to the Czechoslovak pavilion found extraordinary glass sculptures on a monumental scale, executed with superb technical skill. The work of Libenský and his wife, Jaroslava Brychtová, was represented, as was that of René Roubíček. Western artists were awed by what they saw.

In the sixties, glass artists in Czechoslovakia turned their attention to architecture. Between its golden spires and medieval towers, the Prague skyline acquired modern landmarks sheathed in surfaces of glass. A "Glass in Architecture" department was created in the Bratislava Academy of Fine Arts, and Václav Cigler was named to run it. Cigler, whose main field was optical and prismatic glass, trained the first wave of modern glass artists in Slovakia, including Askold Žáčko, who replaced him as department head in 1975.

Transparent, minimalistic, geometric sculptures exploiting glass's prismatic qualities dominated the seventies. The 1980s witnessed an explosion of young talent as Libenský's efforts to propagate a multi-media approach bore fruit. Artists such as Jaroslav Róna, Ivan Mareš, Jiří Nekovář, Ivana Mašitová, Michal Machat, Martin Velíšek, Zdeněk Lhotský, and Ivana Šrámková-Šolcová rebelled against traditional glass forms. Playing down the properties of glass as such, they used it instead as a background for painting and collage, or as an opaque material for sculpture. More recently, glass has been mixed with other media, such as metal, bronze, ceramics, and wood. One contemporary group of artists uses plate and window glass as if it were stretched canvas.

Czech and Slovak artists are routinely invited to take part in international glass exhibitions, and their work is sought after by museums all over the world. They often go abroad to lecture, teach, and write about their work, particularly since the 1989 revolution lifted restrictions on Czechoslovak citizens' right to travel. Their most active followers are in the United States, Japan, Germany, Italy, England, France, the Netherlands, and Scandinavia. Like the collectors, gallery owners, and museum curators, the glass artists in these countries are keen to keep in touch with developments in Czech and Slovak studio glass.

Yet much of the art world still considers glass sculpture a craft rather than a fine art. As a result, outstanding artistic achievements in this non-traditional medium continue to be placed in museums of decorative arts next to weavings and pottery, rather than where they really belong - alongside the Alexander Calders and Henry Moores.

"Invest in glass" was the message of this advertisement, which went up on Czechoslovak billboards in 1992. Photographer: Petr Mazanec.

SINCE THE VELVET REVOLUTION

SINCE the collapse of communism in late 1989, the Czech and Slovak glass industries have had to think long and hard about where they are going. Most of the glassworks are sorely in need of repair and renovation. Many are stymied by limited production capacities, but simply don't have the capital to modernize and expand output. Still others lack export personnel with the language skills and know-how to deal effectively on the international marketplace, now that the factories no longer are forced to sell through state-controlled export channels. Orders from the Soviet Union halted almost overnight, leaving some producers without a market for their goods. Energy costs have risen at a steady pace since 1989. The result has been a sharp decline in glass production.

As soon as a property restitution law was passed, descendants of the prewar owners of some enterprises came forward to claim the factories' return. Other glassworks were placed on the auction block or put up for bidding in public tenders. Most have become joint-stock companies, with their shares divided between pension funds, employees, and private companies. Under various privatization schemes, the monolithic state glass corporations are gradually splitting up, and the small factories they once oversaw are going private.

Sklo Union, the sheet glass producer in Teplice, formed a joint venture with the giant Belgian glass company *Glaverbel*, and currently goes by the name *Glavunion*. A number of glassworks are still waiting to learn what their future status will

INVESTUJTE DO SKLA !
INVESTIČNÍ PRIVATIZAČNÍ FOND
BOHEMIA CRYSTAL
IČO 44 52 0000
BOHEMIA Crystal
MADE IN CZECHOSLOVAKIA

be. Since it is unclear whether their glass output will double in a year's time or be suspended altogether, planning has been virtually impossible.

Glassworks with more secure prospects have shaken up their production lines. The current betting is on nostalgia. The *Rückl* factory in Nižbor is putting out romantic crystal perfume bottles with silk-fringe atomizers and Art Deco sets similar to the ones it made in the 1930s. *Desná* has revived its gentle frosted-glass figurines from the turn of the century. A retired glassblower at another *Rückl* works, in Včelnička, found an original sample book of the factory's designs from 1915 in an attic. It was dusted off, and its colorful ideas are now being incorporated into production. It is almost as if producers are looking back to their roots for inspiration and guidance, picking up where they left off half a century ago.

Many glassblowers have quit their factory jobs and launched out on their own, building furnaces and specializing in decorative glass styles which the larger factories don't produce, such as medieval glass and Art Nouveau. Others are busy moonlighting: they work at the factory during the day and then come home to blow glass under their own private label.

Since the 1989 revolution, at least two brand-new glasshouses and several privately-owned cutting and decorating workshops have joined the ranks of Czech producers. A few foreign companies have moved in to take advantage of Czech glassmaking skills and low labor costs. A grandson of Stefan Rath, the last owner of the famous *J.& L. Lobmeyr Co.* in Kamenický Šenov, returned to the town of his ancestors in 1993 to start up a new company producing elaborately decorated luxury crystal. The engravers working for him include descendants of the highly skilled artisans employed by his grandfather.

WHAT'S IN STORE FOR THE FUTURE?

THE NEXT few years will be a crucial test for the glass industries of the newly independent Czech and Slovak Republics, which succeeded the federal state in January 1993. Can the factories muster their traditional resourcefulness and respond to the latest Western trends? How will they cope with foreign competition on their home turf? Foreign-made glass, unavailable in Czechoslovakia for four decades, is now slowly making its way into the department stores. Low-priced French and Italian table sets are hurting domestic producers, which used to be able to count at least on their own market if foreign orders dwindled.

Can they create attractive enough working conditions to prevent their skilled workers from taking better-paid jobs in Western Europe? Even at home the booming private sector is stealing prized personnel away from large, long-established works, with the result that some factories have simply lost the ability to produce many of the wares on display in their own showrooms.

These challenges come at a time when glass manufacturers

worldwide are struggling, as the best markets for glass - Japan, the United States, and the European Union - are in a recession.

Many Czech and Slovak glass producers, having lost their traditional Soviet and East European markets, will be forced to introduce major changes into their production lines or face the prospect of going bankrupt. Labor costs will rise and push prices higher, thus eliminating one of the competitive advantages long enjoyed by Czech and Slovak glass manufacturers.

Some experts predict a gradual shrinking of the Czech and Slovak glass industries, the result of declining world demand and the market inroads made by automated producers in Western Europe and the Far East. Machine-made glass is already available that is so perfect that it is almost impossible to distinguish from the handmade variety. According to this scenario, only the most prestigious Czech and Slovak producers catering to a select luxury clientele will survive in the decades to come.

But many factors point to a more optimistic outlook. Foremost among them is the existence of a pool of young design talent that is just reaching the peak of their creativity. There are now more Czech and Slovak glass designers, producing a broader range of innovative models, than at any other time in this century. Raw materials for glassmaking are still cheap and plentiful, and the indispensable ingredients of tradition, technique, and business acumen are all present in abundance. The first sparks of innovation can already be seen in the stemware of some of Bohemia's newer glassworks and those that have recently gone private. Furthermore, Czechs and Slovaks are well positioned geographically to exploit the huge market potential to the east.

The glassmaking industries in Bohemia and Slovakia have always prospered when given the freedom to do so, and the coming era should prove no exception.

A HISTORICAL CONTRIBUTION TO GLASSMAKING

I F ONE WERE to single out the greatest overall contribution of the Bohemian glass industry to the development of glassmaking, it would undoubtedly be the inexhaustible inventiveness of its designers. From the 16th to the 20th century, glass masters in Bohemia created scores of different colors, shapes, styles, and glass types, constantly taking the development of glass as an artistic medium in new directions. Glassmakers in Slovakia also came up with original design ideas, but as a general rule they concentrated more on producing functional glass for daily use than on elaborate decoration. Since the 1950s, Czech and Slovak artistic creativity has been channeled primarily into studio glass rather than tableware, although in the future increasing market pressure is likely to lead to innovations in household glass design as well.

The influence of Bohemian glassmaking traditions has spread through the migration of skilled craftsmen from the 17th century onwards to the farthest corners of Europe in search of work or higher wages. This talent drain resumed in 1990, once again depleting domestic factories of valuable personnel.

Once settled in Germany, Austria, France, the Netherlands, Sweden, Argentina, Ireland, or England, Bohemian glassmakers passed on their well-honed techniques to the firms in their adopted country. Some of the world's most famous Western glass manufacturers owe their success in no small part to artisans trained in Bohemia. The *Swarovski* company, for example, Austria's preeminent crystal producer, was established in 1895 by Daniel Swarovski, an inventor from the costume jewelry center of *Gablonz* (Jablonec nad Nisou). A colony of Bohemian glass engravers worked in Stourbridge, England, and at the *Orrefors* company in Sweden before World War I. The founders of Ireland's *Waterford Crystal* enlisted the help of Bohemian-born cutters and glassblowers, and Miroslav Havel, a native Czech, was the firm's chief designer for 25 years.

Another field in which Bohemian producers set world standards was in glass costume jewelry. Before companies in *Gablonz* (Jablonec nad Nisou) made glittering glass gems available to the general public in the latter half of the nineteenth century, jewelry had been the exclusive domain of the rich.

Bohemia also played a role in the development of sheet glass. Although the Romans are believed to have invented glass window-panes, window glass was made in Bohemia as far back as the 10th century, and in far greater quantities than in other European lands. Up until the end of the 17th century, windows were made of round glass discs (roundels) soldered together with strips of lead. In the 18th century, Bohemian works were producing

the largest panes of glass in Central Europe, although the Belgians later improved upon their method.

The French engineer Émile Fourcault invented a technique for making continuously drawn sheet

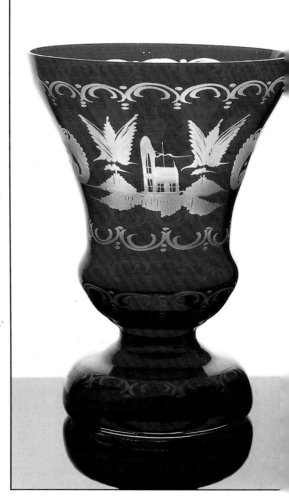

glass and, after being rebuffed in Belgium, came to Bohemia to try it out. A factory in the town of Hostonice u Bíliny adopted it in 1919, leading to a dramatic increase in regional sheet glass production. The same method is used in modified form today in most of the world's largest sheet glass plants. The largest glassworks on the territory of the former Czechoslovakia is the Teplice-based *Glavunion*, which manufactures on the order of 1,000 tons of sheet glass a day.

In 1938, Czechoslovakia was one of the world's top three producers of household glass. Half a century later, it ranked seventh in volume of glass exports, after West Germany, France, the United States, Belgium, Italy, and Great Britain. By 1992, its transformation from a centrally-planned to a free-market economy in full swing, it had slipped down to 14th place.

Czech and Slovak glass now competes for shelf space with the glass exports of at least 25 other nations. Yet many factors combine to make it unique in the market.

Probably nowhere else in the world is there such a high concentration of glass manufacturers making exclusive drinking sets by hand, nor as wide a variety of styles in production.

According to government statistics, the Czechoslovak glass and costume jewelry industries employed 25,000 workers at the end of 1992, out of a total population of 15 million. Glass exports, covering about 60% of glass production, totaled USD $344.6 million. The United States exported double that amount - but then, the former Czechoslovakia was roughly the size of North Carolina. Moreover, export volume is likely to grow as market reforms take root.

The most exciting area to watch will be studio glass. Czech and Slovak artists are currently at the forefront of international trends. As the doyen of Czech art glass, Stanislav Libenský, once put it, a nation's glass often reflects the state of its society. If political and economic change continues as expected, glass can look forward to a renaissance in the new Republics.

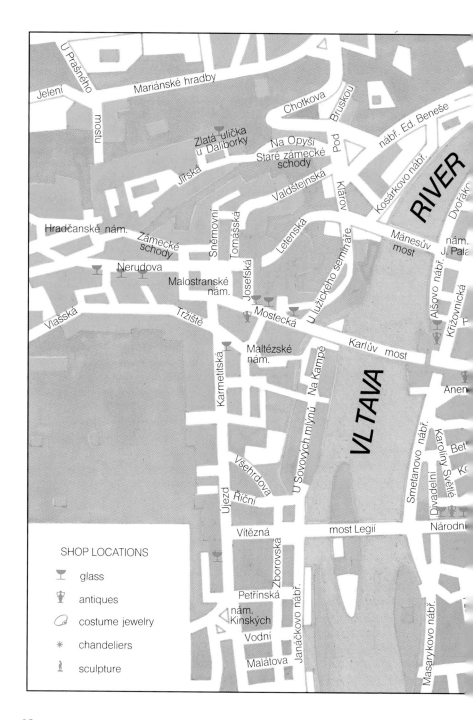

SHOP LOCATIONS

- 🍸 glass
- 🏺 antiques
- 🪔 costume jewelry
- ✳ chandeliers
- 🗿 sculpture

PART FOUR • SHOPPING FOR GLASS

WHERE TO FIND THE BEST BARGAINS

PRAGUE is still the best place to shop for glass in the former Czechoslovakia - not only for the sheer number of stores but also because they offer the greatest diversity in glassware and the highest level of quality. But many new shops are also sprouting up in other popular tourist destinations, especially the Czech spa towns of Karlovy Vary and Mariánské Lázně, and the Slovak capital, Bratislava.

For glass shops on the main tourist routes in the Czech capital - crisscrossing the Old Town between Wenceslas Square (Václavské náměstí) and Charles Bridge - opening hours are generally 9am-7pm, seven days a week. Off the beaten track, shops usually close at 11am on Saturdays, if they are open at all during the weekend. On full working days, some shops close for lunch for an hour or two at midday.

As in any city, the shops in the historical center tend to be the most expensive. If you're looking for bargains, seek out the places where the locals themselves are likely to shop - out of the center and off the major thoroughfares.

The department stores are a good bet. *Kotva*, Prague's largest, has an interesting selection on the second floor at prices well below what they would be in and around Old Town Square. You might find pieces here from *Harrachov, Český Křišťál, Karolinka, Katarínska Huta*, and other impor-

tant manufacturers, but quality varies and supplies are limited. You can have your glass engraved while you wait at a small booth at the entrance to the glass department. There is also a special *Crystalex* boutique on the fourth floor, although its selection is rather nar-

row. *Kotva* is the huge modern building at the corner of Revoluč-ní ulice and Náměstí Republiky.

Diamant is another department store with a large glass section, also in the low- to medium-price range. Diamant is near the bottom end of Wenceslas Square, on the left side of the street as you look up towards the National Museum. To reach the glass department, climb the stairs on the left just inside the entrance.

If you're in the market for top-quality glass and see a piece you like, snap it up without delay, since you might not see it anywhere else. The price is bound to be far less than what you would pay for the same item in New York or London, and the selection of pieces in a particular pattern - for example, a pitcher, a decanter, four shapes of stemware - will be incomparably larger. When it comes to the more exclusive brands, keep in mind that their manufacturers are not always able to produce enough to meet demand, so supplies may be limited.

There is no best time to shop, except perhaps off-season or in April or May, when the stores have had time to stock up on inventory and are not so jammed with buyers.

The *Moser* shop window at Na příkopě 12 in central Prague. Photographer: Diane Foulds.

The recently renovated mahogany interior in the Prague *Moser* shop. Photo: Moser Co., Ltd.

The best selection is found in the shops geared to foreign customers, as domestic demand for expensive lines is limited. By the same token, while the less flashy stores offer cheaper prices, they also carry less exclusive wares.

If you're bent on a specific label, look up the manufacturer under "The Major Glassworks" (part Five) to see if it has a retail outlet in Prague. The well-known factories such as *Moser* often have more than one store. Prices get better the closer you are to the factory. *Moser's* Prague store sells only the very best; second-quality items may go for 10% less at the Karlovy Vary factory or store. They've usually been marked down for flaws that the layman would never be able to detect, for example if a wine glass is ever so slightly thicker or thinner than the norm.

Regrettably, the concept of sale merchandise is still relatively unknown in this part of the world, especially when it comes to anything even vaguely related to the tourist trade. The assumption is that if anyone can afford it, it is the Western visitor, and in a sense, it's true. Even stemware priced for the domestic market is often a luxury for the Czech or Slovak consumer. Moreover,

retailers do not add the high margins that Western stores do, so there is no room for large-scale discounting. Retail margins usually range between 30-50%.

Glass is widely sold from street stands on Wenceslas Square and Charles Bridge. You shouldn't write these stands off. Sometimes they sell name brands, sometimes the work of small, private ateliers. Sidewalk vendors don't usually grant refunds or exchanges, so check glass closely for flaws and bubbles before you buy. For that matter, always unwrap and examine every piece of a set you buy before the sales assistant rings it up.

True glass fanatics determined to get value for money should make an effort to visit Nový Bor. This lively town, about a two-hour drive north of Prague, is full of glass shops priced well below those in the capital. The headquarters of *Crystalex* and *Egermann-Exbor* are both in Nový Bor, and both have shops in the center of town. It's best to arrive early, do some leisurely shopping, and leave enough time to wander through the Nový Bor Glass Museum, which is right on the main square. The museum also sells a small amount of glass.

THE BEST SHOPS

Crystalex
Classic styles, colored, painted, and cut glass, about 20% modern. Moderate prices. Malé náměstí 6, Prague 1. Tel. (02) 24 22 84 59. Open daily 9am-6pm, Sat. 10am-4pm. Credit cards.

Crystalex
Contemporary. Karlovo náměstí 6, Prague 2. Moderate prices. Tel. (02) 29 12 60. Open Mon. - Fri. 9am-6pm, Sat. till 1pm. Cash only.

Moser
Exclusive. Mostly classic. Expensive. Na příkopě 12, Prague 1. Tel. (02) 24 21 12 93. Open Mon. – Fri. 9am-7pm, Sat. till 2pm. Credit cards, shipping service.

Jafa
Judaica, costume jewelry, *Moser* crystal, designer glass. Moderate prices. Maiselova 15, Prague 1. Tel. (02) 231 00 40. Open daily 9am-7pm. Credit cards, currency exchange office, shipping service.

Salon Philadelphia
24% lead cut crystal by *Glassworks Bohemia,* Poděbrady. Costume jewelry, art glass. Moderate prices. Vodičkova 30, Prague 1. Tel. (02) 235 84 42. Open Mon.-Sat. 9am-7pm. Credit cards, currency exchange office, shipping service.

Sklo Bohemia
Company store. 24% lead cut crystal. Moderate prices. Na příkopě 17, Prague 1. Tel. (02) 24 21 16 69. Open daily, 9am-7pm. Credit cards, currency exchange office.

Diamant
Stemware, paperweights, figurines. Fairly large selection. Inexpensive to moderate prices. Václavské náměstí 3, Prague 1. Tel. (02) 24 21 04 75. Open Mon.- Fri. 9am-7pm, Sat. till 3pm.

Kotva
Stemware, bowls, vases, paperweights, etc. Inexpensive to moderate prices. Náměstí Republiky 8, Prague 1. Tel. (02) 24 80 11 11. Open Mon.- Fri. 8am-7pm, Thurs. till 8pm, Sat. till 4pm. Credit cards, currency exchange office.

Contrans
Contemporary, cut lead crystal, costume jewelry. Moderate prices. Malé náměstí 1, Prague 1. Tel. (02) 26 23 13. Open daily 10am-7pm. Credit cards.

HB Bohemia Crystal
Classic and contemporary cut glass, moderate prices. Celetná 5, Prague 1. Tel. (02) 23 29 972. Open daily, 9am-7pm. Credit cards, shipping service.

Dana
Historical and contemporary stemware, porcelain. Národní třída 43 and Perlová 10, Prague 1. Tel. (02) 24 21 46 55 Mon.-Fri. 9am-7pm, Sat. till 6pm, Sun. 11am-6pm. Credit cards.

Egermann-Exbor
Red-stain glass, historical reproductions, contemporary, glass flowers. Moderate

prices. Na příkopě 13 and
Národní 17, Prague 1.
Open daily 9am-7pm.
Credit cards, shipping service.

Mercuria Morava
Moser crystal. Expensive.
Kobližná 10. Tel. (05) 42 21 33 28.
Open Mon.-Fri. 9am-6pm, Sat.
8am-12pm. American Express.

Glass Market
Květná and *Karolinka* glass,
cut lead crystal, chandeliers.
Moderate. Orlí 9.
Tel. (05) 42 21 21 90. Open Mon.-
Fri. 9am-6pm, Sat. till 1pm.
Cash only.

Crystal
Lednické Rovne and
Crystalex glass, cut lead
crystal, chandeliers.
Radnická 9. Tel. (05) 42 21 02
39. Open Mon.-Fri. 9am-6pm,
Sat. till 11am. Credit cards.

Moser
Moser crystal in the original
shop. Stará louka 40.
Tel. (017) 32 24 469. Open Mon.-
Fri. 9am-5pm. Credit cards,
shipping service.

Madonna
A broad variety of classic and
contemporary. Lázeňská 7/23.
Tel. (017) 298 32. Open daily
9:30am- 6pm. Credit cards.

Egermann-Exbor
Classic *Egermann* colored glass.
Stará louka 50.
Tel. (017) 252 73. Open daily
9am-7pm. Credit cards.

Cristallicka
Karolinka glass. Stará louka 63.
Tel. (017) 242 77. Open daily
10am-6pm. Cash only.

Madonna
Costume jewelry, cut lead
crystal, contemporary, and colored
glass. Hlavní 228. Tel. (0165)
4755. Open daily
9am-9pm. Credit cards.

Bohemia Glass
Egermann glass, high enamel,
costume jewelry, paneled glass.
Hlavní 60. Tel. (0165) 5864. Open
daily 9am-7pm. Credit cards.

Silvie

Poděbrady 24% lead cut crystal, contemporary stemware from *Vrbno* and *Lednické Rovne*. Hlavní 232. Tel. (0165) 3046. Open daily 9:30am-6pm. Credit cards.

R & H

Chřibská, Karolinka, and other glass, costume jewelry. Hlavní 319. Tel. (0165) 3190. Open daily 9am-6pm. Credit cards.

IN BRATISLAVA:

Toreza

Moser crystal. Expensive. Rybárska brána 2. Tel. (07) 33 02 60. Open Mon.-Fri. 9:30am-6pm, Sat. 9am-1pm. Credit cards.

Michel-Glascentrum

Slovak glass and chandeliers. Inexpensive to moderate. Obchodná 44. Tel. (07) 33 49 73. Open Mon.-Fri. 9am-6pm, Sat. till 4pm. Cash only.

The classic flute-cut design of the "Jubilant" drinking set by *Moser* is a company hallmark. Photo: *Moser Co., Ltd.*

Bios

Chandeliers. Next to the Hotel Forum at Suché Mýto 19. Tel. (07) 201 11 36. Open Mon.-Fri. 9am-5pm, Sat. till 12pm. Eurocard, Mastercard.

Koral

High enamel, cut glass, costume jewelry, chandeliers. Rybárska brána 1. Open Mon.-Fri. 9am-6pm, Sat. till 1pm. Cash only.

Franc Agentur

Lednické Rovne glass. Štefánikova 3. Tel. (07) 33 21 30. Open Mon.-Fri. 10am-6pm, Sat. 8am-12pm.

Sklo-Porcelán

Lower- to medium-priced Czech and Slovak glass. Hlavné námestie 6. Tel. (07) 33 55 10. Open Mon. 11am-6pm, Tues.-Fri. 9am-6pm, Sat. 9am-1pm. Cash only.

Bohemia

Lower- to medium-priced Czech and Slovak glass. Poštová 3. Open Mon.-Fri. 10am-6pm. Tel. (07) 32 34 67.

SPECIALTY STORES

LISTED below are the best places to find glass jewelry and buttons, chandeliers, antique glass, and designer glass in Prague. As of this writing, there's nowhere to buy loose beads for those interested in stringing their own necklaces. Nor are there any stores specializing in glass Christmas tree ornaments, but these can be found (seasonally) at the department store *Kotva*.

GLASS JEWELRY:

Royal
The widest costume jewelry
selection in the country. Ask
to see the jewelry in the
drawers under the counter.
Na příkopě 12, Prague 1.
Tel. (02) 24 21 05 52. Open Mon.-
Sat. 9am-7pm, Sun. 10am-7pm.
Traveler's checks, credit cards.

Rapa
Na poříčí 13, Prague 1.
Tel. (02) 231 47 16.
Open Mon.-Fri. 9am-7pm,
Sat. till 2pm. Credit cards.

Bijouterie Boutique
V jámě 5, Prague 1.
Tel. 21 42 20 89. Open Mon.-
Fri. 10am-2pm, 2:30pm-6pm,
Sat.-Sun. till 2pm. Cash only.

Krone
The jewelry is on the ground
floor in the back. On Wenceslas
Square, corner of
Jindřišská ulice, Prague 1.
Tel. (02) 24 23 04 77. Open Mon.-
Fri. 8am-7pm, Sat. till 6pm,
Sun. 9am-6pm.

Kotva
The jewelry is on the ground
floor to the right.
Náměstí Republiky 8, Prague 1.
Tel. (02) 24 80 11 11. Open Mon.-
Fri. 8am-7pm, Thurs. till 8pm,
Sat. till 4pm. Credit cards.

GLASS BUTTONS:

Maro
Near the Palmovka metro stop
at Na žertvách 6, 180 00 Prague 8.
Open Mon.-Fri. 9am-6pm.

CHANDELIERS:

Luna
Na příkopě 16, Prague 1.
Tel. (02) 24 21 12 82. Open Mon.-
Fri. 10am-6pm, Sat. 9am-1pm.
Credit cards.

Lustry
Kamenický Šenov chandeliers.
Jindřišská 17, Prague 1.
Tel. (02) 26 83 86. Open Mon.-
Fri. 9:30am-6:30pm,
Sat. 8am-3pm.
Credit cards.

Linie
Kamenický Šenov chandeliers.
Jungmannova 27, Prague 1.
Tel. (02) 26 23 94. Open Mon.-
Fri. 10am-7pm, Sat. till 5pm,
Sun. till 3pm. Credit cards.

Bohemia Glas
Kozí ul. 9, Prague 1.
Tel. (02) 24 81 16 71. Open daily
10am-6pm. Credit cards.

Glas Shop
Jindřišská 29, Prague 1.
Tel. (02) 24 21 34 85. Open Mon.-
Fri. 9am-4pm, Sat. 10am-4pm.
Credit cards.

Světlo Lux
Národní třída 25, Prague 1.
Tel. (02) 236 54 29. Open Mon.-
Fri. 9am-7pm, Sat. 10am-5pm.

DESIGNER GLASS:

Dialog Art
Near Náměstí Republiky at
Hybernská 1, Prague 1.
Tel. (02) 235 64 35. Open Mon.-
Fri. 10am- 8pm, Sat.-Sun. until
5pm. Credit cards.

Melissa
Off Old Town Square at
Pařížská 3, Prague 1.
Tel. (02) 232 58 06. Open Mon.-
Wed., Sun. 9am-9pm, Thurs.-Sat.
till 11pm. Credit cards.

ANTIQUES

SOME of the most beautiful (and expensive) Bohemian crystal is sitting in the windows of Prague's glittering antique stores. These shops are in constant contact with the Museum of Decorative Arts, which documents all incoming pieces before they reach the shelf. If you buy an antique, have the shopkeeper give you an export permit and a purchase receipt, and make sure they bear the shop's stamp. Without these documents, the antique may be confiscated at the border. Export permits are usually valid for three months. If you won't be leaving the country within that period, you will have to take the permit to the Museum of Decorative Arts to have the validity extended. The person to see there is either Mrs. Rubešová or Mr. Kočí. It's best to call in advance and make an appointment (Wednesdays only, 9am-12pm, 2pm-4pm). The museum is across the street from the Rudolfinum concert hall at 17 listopadu 2, Prague 1. Tel. (02) 24 81 12 41.

It is a criminal offense to take antiques out of the Czech or Slovak Republics without an export permit. Unfortunately, there is no set law defining an antique, as classification has as much to do with type as with age. Each article is considered on its own merits.

The stringency has its justification: since Czechoslovakia's borders were opened in 1989, countless irreplaceable pieces have disappeared from homes, museums, and churches, smuggled out to antique dealers in the West. The authorities are waging a desperate battle to salvage what few vintage art treasures are left.

A word to the wise: Don't risk a purchase unless the shopkeeper produces the required export permit. If instead the shopkeeper tells you not to worry, keep in mind that the store is not liable for what it sells. If you're caught, the antique will be confiscated and your money will not be refunded.

One possible solution is to take a few pictures of the desired piece and have a replica made. Companies specializing in reproductions are: *Glassco*, Svatoborská 23, CZ-697 01 Kyjov. Tel./Fax (0631) 9421 59; and *S.B.K.*, Mírová 69, CZ-471 24 Mimoň. Tel./Fax (0425) 620 29.

ANTIQUE SHOPS:

Starožitnosti
Mostecká 7, Prague 1.
Tel. (02) 5314 83.
Open daily 10am-6pm.

Antique Jan Huněk
Pařížská 1, Prague 1.
Tel. (02) 232 36 04.
Open daily 10am-7pm. Credit cards.

Antique Andrle
Next to Charles Bridge at Křížovnická 1, Prague 1.

Tel. (02) 231 16 25. Open Mon.-Thurs. 10am-6pm, Fri.-Sat. till 8pm. Credit cards.

Starožitnosti Dinand
Národní 36-38, Prague 1.
Tel. 26 00 34. Open
Mon.-Fri. 10am-12pm,
1pm-4pm. Credit cards.

Kůrka a Komárek
Železná 10, Prague 1.
Tel. (02) 26 06 25
Open Mon. - Fri. 10am-6pm, Sat. 10am-2pm.

The Glass Trading Centre in Liberec, housing the vast *Glassexport* showroom. Photo: *Glassexport*. Photographers: Zdenka Kalabisová and Antonín Krčmář.

GETTING THROUGH CUSTOMS

A S OF JANUARY 1993, all gifts and personal items can be taken out of the Czech and Slovak Republics duty-free as long as they are not intended for commercial resale. This includes your glass purchases.

If you send glass through the mail, you must go to the Customs post office at Plzeňská 139, Prague 5 (Smíchov district). Tel. (02) 24 51 17 54. Open Mon.-Fri. 7am-3pm. To get there, take tram 4, 7, or·9 to the Kavalírka stop. Then follow the tram tracks back to the six-storey blue building behind you. The post office is straight ahead as you walk in. Be sure you've brought all sales receipts with you. If you're shipping an antique, you'll need an export permit from the shop.

It's worth the extra cost to have the store ship your glass for you. They know how to pack it and they will save you the time and trouble of taking it to Customs. What's more, they will insure the item and replace it if it does arrive damaged. Be sure to obtain a written guarantee against breakage, and ask about the procedures to follow in order to have your glass replaced.

If you are exporting glass for resale, you may need to use the services of a freight forwarder, customs broker, trading company, or some other locally registered intermediary. The following firms provide exporting services:

Glassexport -
Třída 1. máje 52,
CZ-461 74 Liberec.
Tel. (048) 31 51 11, Fax 4210 27.

Jablonex -
Costume jewelry. Palackého 41,
CZ-466 37 Jablonec nad Nisou.
Tel. (0428) 40 11 11, Fax 273 62.

THE VALUE-ADDED TAX

IN JANUARY 1993, both the Czech and Slovak Republics introduced a value-added tax, or VAT (in Czech, *Daň z přidané hodnoty*, or DPH). This tax, which is something like a sales tax, adds an extra 22% to the price of consumer grassware between the time it leaves the factory and when it enters the retail shop. The laws were loosely modeled on the German VAT system. Unlike in Germany, however, Czech and Slovak authorities have not yet worked out a way to refund the VAT to non-resident foreigners who take their purchases out of the country. This is likely to change at some point, but for the time being, there is no way to avoid paying VAT unless you are buying large quantities of glass and shipping in bulk.

THE MAJOR GLASSWORKS

▲ glassworks

○ W

Dresden ○

Chřibská

Kamenický Šenov

Liberec

Dubí u Teplic

Harrachov

Nový Bor

Železný Brod

Koštany   Teplice

Turnov

Libochovice

Nový Bydžov

Karlovy Vary

Hradec Králové

PRAGUE

Vrbno pod

Nižbor

Poděbrady

Plzeň

Litomyšl

Tasice

CZECH REPUBLIC

Josefodol

Světlá nad Sázavou

Heřmanova Hut

Skrdlovice

Úsobrno

Vala

Antonínův Důl

GERMANY

Včelnička

Brno

Rosice u Brna

České Budějovice

Kyjov

Lenora

Chlum u Třeboně

Passau ○

Munich ○

○ Linz

VIENNA ■

Salzburg ○

AUSTRIA

DETAIL

Jizerka ○

Kristiánov

Bedřichov
○

Josefův Důl

Janov nad Nisou

Harrachov

Liberec

Lučany

Desná

Smržovka

Tanvald ○

Jablonec
nad Nisou

Zásada

Železný Brod

POLAND

○ Kraków

ava ■

Karolinka

○
Bardejov

Medzilaborce

Lednické Rovne

Nemšová

SLOVAKIA

■ Košice

○
Užgorod

Banská Bystrica ■

Utekáč

Zlatno

Málinec

Katarínska Huta

Poltár

ava

VA

HUNGARY

UKRAINE

ROMANIA

■ BUDAPEST

73

PART FIVE • THE MAJOR GLASSWORKS

I F YOU'RE interested in seeing how glass is made, it's well worth planning a trip to at least one of the leading factories. You can get a feel for what goes into the manufacturing process, and also pick up some bargains at the factory store, where prices may be anywhere from 5% to 40% lower than in Prague.

Reaching the factories is easiest by car. On the way you're likely to pass through rolling countryside dotted with castles and old towns with picturesque main squares. When you arrive in the town where your target factory is located, just aim for the tallest smokestack.

The Czech glass industry is largely concentrated in northern Bohemia, about a two-hour drive from Prague. The four "glass capitals" are Nový Bor, Jablonec nad Nisou, Kamenický Šenov, and Železný Brod. Each of these towns has a museum and glassmaking school, and there are numerous glassworks nearby.

The city of Liberec is worth a special trip. The imposing white castle on Felberova street in the center of town houses the wholesale showroom of the leading glass trading company in Central Europe, *Glassexport Co., Ltd.* With 30,000 samples on display, the Bohemia Crystal Trade Centre is the largest glass showroom in the world. Unfortunately, it is not open to the public. But do visit the outstanding glass collection in the Museum of Northern Bohemia (see "Museums" in Part Six).

The 50 most important glass producers in the Czech and Slovak Republics are listed here alphabetically by location. Names of stores where the factory's products can be purchased are provided, and opening hours are given.

Company labels are reproduced to enable you to identify the glass you see in the shops. All glassware exported through *Glassexport* is labeled with the protected trademark "Bohemia Glass" or "Bohemia Crystal," on an oval sticker with two crossed arrows curving upwards. Sometimes it will also bear the label of the individual producer. The *Jablonex* trading company, formerly the state's sole exporter of costume jewelry, uses the trademark "Bijoux de Bohême." A white label with the Roman numeral II indicates that the item is a second.

Some manufacturers are happy to let individuals watch the glassblowers at work. Others only permit group tours booked in advance, while a few actively discourage any contact with the public. This information is provided under "Visits." If you're driving a long way to shop at a particular factory store, it would be wise to phone ahead to confirm that it will be open. Most factories and their retail outlets shut down for three to four weeks at the end of July. If you'd prefer to go with a group, the following travel agencies offer excursions:

Čedok - Tours to the *Tasice* factory ("Secrets of Bohemian Glass Production") from April 8-Oct. 28. Participants can try blowing glass themselves. Na příkopě 18, Rytířská 16, Pařížská 6, Prague 1. Tel. (02) 24 19 76 42, 26 36 97, 231 25 81, 231 82 55, Fax 232 16 56.

American Express Travel Office - Tours to *Sklárny Bohemia* at Poděbrady and other factories. Václavské náměstí 56, Prague 1. Tel. (02) 24 22 77 87, 26 65 29. Open Mon.-Fri. 9am-6pm, Sat. till 12pm.

Duo Travel - Individual or group tours to any glassworks requested. Novomlýnská 2, Prague 1. Tel. (02) 231 73 16. Open Mon.-Fri. 9am-3pm.

Intensive Travel - Individual or group tours to any glassworks requested. Revoluční 13, Prague 1. Tel. (02) 286 33 18. Open Mon.-Fri. 10am-6pm.

One final word: Don't forget to bring cash, as few shops outside Prague and other tourist centers accept credit cards or traveler's checks. Unless otherwise noted, the factory and retail outlets listed under "Stores" only take cash.

ANTONÍNŮV DŮL

Jihlava Glassworks
(Jihlavské sklárny)
CZ-330 24 Jihlava

Tel. (066) 255 41
Fax   4637
Telex 68300

THE WORKS at *Antonínův Důl* near Jihlava is one of the few glassmaking enterprises in this hilly region of central Bohemia that have survived since the 19th century. The name of the site - *důl* comes from *údolí,* meaning "valley" - highlights the fact that it was once common to build glass factories at the lowest point in a forested valley, near a river, where there was plenty of water to keep the moulds wet, facilitate the glass-blowing process, and put out fires.

Antonínův Důl, also called *Antonínodol*, was founded in 1845 by K. A. Ascherl. It went through a succession of owners until its nationalization in 1945,

when it was merged with other nearby plants and glass-cutting workshops specializing in cut lead crystal. The new conglomerate, *Sklárny Bohemia*, also comprised the factory at *Dobronín*, the decorating workshops at *Úsobí* and *Brodce*, and later the *Poděbrady* works, where *Sklárny Bohemia* now has its headquarters.

Dobronín was founded by Josef Inwald, the owner of several other Bohemian glassworks, in 1876. Production expanded rapidly. On the eve of World War I, the factory employed 400 glassmakers. In the mid-1940s, *Dobronín* produced lead crystal fashioned by Ludvika Smrčková, one of the most influential designers of the postwar era. After its nationalization, the works was reorganized as the *Dobronínské sklárny* (Dobronín Glassworks), until it joined *Antonínův Důl* and ultimately came under the administration of *Poděbrady.*

In 1993, *Antonínův Důl, Dobronín,* and the cutting workshops in *Úsobí* and *Brodce* broke away from *Poděbrady* and formed the private joint-stock company *Jihlavské sklárny* (Jihlava Glassworks). The aim is to continue producing handmade 24% lead cut crystal, with an emphasis on modernistic, one-of-a-kind artistic pieces.

Visits: Visitors are welcome to stop in at either of the two factories if they phone in advance.

Stores: In Jihlava, *Bohemia* - The company showroom and shop. Matky boží 6.
Tel. (066) 204 98.
Open Mon.-Fri. 8am-12pm, 2pm-6pm, Sat. 9am-12pm.

In Prague, *Salon Philadelphia* - Vodičkova 30, Prague 1.
Tel. (02) 235 84 42. Open Mon.-Sat. 9am-7pm.

Photographer: Miroslav Vojtěchovský.

Photo: *Crystalex*

CHLUM U TŘEBONĚ
Crystalex-Český křišťál
CZ - *378 04* Chlum u Třeboně
Tel. (0333) 974 11
Fax   972 13

THIS GLASSWORKS, the youngest in southern Bohemia, is the favorite of many crystal connoisseurs thanks to its chief designer, Jan Gabrhel. The award-winning artist is best known for his formal dinnerware sets in elegantly sculpted designs

with exquisite flute-cut motifs reminiscent of *Moser.* The distinction is that *Moser* pieces are made of a harder crystal and are all hand-polished, while much of the glass produced by *Český křišťál* has a 10% lead content and is acid-polished. Although purists insist on hand-polishing, for most glass lovers there is no visible difference. If anything, acid-polishing makes the surface look even more perfectly finished than hand-polishing. An additional factor is price: If you adore *Moser* glassware but can't afford it, you should consider *Český křišťál.*

The factory itself was an old ironworks when it was leased in 1891 by *C. Stoelze & Söhne* and converted into a glassworks. Financial problems forced it to close in 1910. It was reopened in 1919 by Václav Hrdina. Sales of its cut and painted hot-shaped glass experienced two boom periods in the 1920s. Following its nationalization in 1945, the factory was eventually consolidated, under the aegis of *Crystalex,* with the works at *Lenora* and the former *Rückl* factory in Kamenice nad Lipou. The latter split off from the troika after the 1989 revolution and was sold to the descendants of its original owners. *Český křišťál* is still attached to Crystalex for the time being, but is no longer associated with *Lenora.*

The company label is an upturned "C" in the shape of a goblet.

Visits: Visitors should phone in advance to watch production. The factory is about an hour's drive southeast of České Budějovice along scenic country roads. Take Rte. E551/34 east through Třeboň and follow the signs south to Suchdol. Chlum u Třeboně nestles amid lakes and forests. You can't miss the plant, located on the far edge of the village; drive slowly and watch for the sign.

Stores: There is a shop at the factory with unbeatable prices. It's directly opposite the entrance to the works.
Tel. (0333) 974 18. Open Mon.-Fri. 8am-3pm.

In Prague, *Crystalex* - Malé náměstí 6, Prague 1. Open daily 9am-7pm. *Bohemia Art Crystal* -

Železná 14, Prague 1. Open Mon.-Sat. 9:30am-7pm, Sun. 1pm-7pm. Traveler's checks. *Diamant* - Václavské náměstí 3, Prague 1. Open Mon.-Fri. 9am-7pm, Sat. till 3pm.

In Třeboň, *Sklárny Český Křišťál* - Husova 13. Tel. (0333) 3965. Open Tues.-Fri. 9am-12pm, 12:30pm-5pm, Sun. 8am-12pm.

CHŘIBSKÁ

Chřibská Glassworks
(Sklárny Chřibská - Black a spol. s.r.o.)
CZ-407 44 Chřibská
Tel. (0413) 913 12
Fax   913 13

S KLÁRNY CHŘIBSKÁ may be the oldest glassworks still operating in Central Europe. Records indicate it was probably founded in 1414 - hence the label, which is a gold sticker bearing that date above a galleon. There is archeological evidence to suggest that glass was produced on the site already 200 years before that.

To reach the historic works requires a long drive through rolling countryside, but the remarkable town of Chřibská alone is worth the effort. With its historic timber houses, the village looks more like a movie set than a factory town. The glass is the second surprise. Far from being tradition-bound, *Chřibská* produces unusual and highly colorful glass in modernistic designs. Its line includes thick-

Photo: *Crystal*
Photographer: Lubomír Hána

and thin-walled vases, bowls, and platters - no stemware - which play optical tricks on you when you try to look through them. All the glass is hot-shaped, meaning that, while still in the molten state, it is shaped into its final form without moulds.

It was at *Chřibská* that the first Bohemian guild of glass painters, engravers, gilders, and borers was founded in 1661. In the next century engravers outnumbered painters.

Ownership of the works passed from the aristocratic Kinský family to J. J. Kittl in 1767. His descendants achieved great success with Empire-style drinking goblets and vases decorated with biscuit enamel, agate staining, and other elaborate finishes. Under the Mayer family, which owned the works from 1882-1945, the emphasis shifted from decoration to color.

Chřibská was nationalized in 1946 and consolidated into the *Borské sklo* corporation, the forerunner of today's *Crystalex* corporation. Josef Hospodka, a glass

designer who was director of the house for three decades, introduced more hot-shaped designs into the production line in the 1950s. Hospodka's style predominated into the late 1980s. But since the 1989 revolution, things have started to change. At the 1993 "Ambiente" glass fair in Frankfurt, *Chřibská* presented some startlingly unconventional designer pieces.

The works became a private company in June 1993. With the likes of talented designer Zdena Jobová on its staff, *Chřibská* will be a producer to watch.

Visits: Visitors are welcome, but it's best to phone in advance.

Stores: There is a shop at the factory. Tel. (0413) 913 12. Open Mon.-Fri. 9am-4pm, Sat.-Sun. till 12pm.

In Prague, *Krystal* - Václavské náměstí 30, Prague 1. Tel. (02) 26 33 84. Open Mon.-Fri. 9am-6pm, Sat. till 4pm. Selected *Chřibská* pieces are carried by the *Kotva* department store.

DESNÁ

Ornela, a.s. - Division Desná Glassworks
(Ornela, a.s. - Divize Desná Sklárna)
CZ-468 61 Desná
v Jizerských horách
Tel. (0428) 694 20-1
Fax   622 18

THE DESNÁ works is the world's largest producer of the colored glass rods needed to manufacture beads, buttons, and figurines. About half of the glass rods it makes are earmarked for the production of rocaille, the tiny "seed" beads used in Native American art.

Desná has been producing glass semifinished products since 1848. It was one of five glassworks owned by Josef Riedel, a 19th-century glass magnate whose family had been in Bohemia since the early 1700s. Riedel was a leading industrialist in the Austro-Hungarian Empire; besides the glass factories, he owned two decorating workshops, a bronze foundry, a cotton mill, and a textile plant. One of his most important contributions to glassmaking was the invention of fluorescent glazes using uranium oxide, which he dubbed *Annagelb* and *Annagrün* after his wife, Anna. The scientific experiments of Josef Riedel, Jr., led to the development of 600 glass colors, which had a tremendous impact on bottle and jewelry production.

Riedel's grandson Walter invented fiberglass and went on to develop large picture tubes that the German Luftwaffe used in aerial surveillance devices in World War II. In 1945, Walter Riedel was arrested by the Soviets and taken to Russia, where he supervised a glass laboratory until his release in 1956.

The Riedels had closed their textile mills before the war, but what was left of their glass empire was nationalized by the Czechoslovak government in 1945. All of the glassworks and glass cutting workshops in the Desná and Lučany region were merged and renamed *Jablonecké sklárny.*

Independent since 1993, *Desná* produces a wide range of articles such as lampshades, microscope lenses and cover glasses, chandelier pendants, tiny glass balls used in milling and in reflective road signs, dental glass, neon tubes, and laboratory microboxes. At the same time, its glassblowers make vases, candle-sticks, and colored crystal paper-weights filled with bubbles. *Desná* recently formed a partnership with *České perličky*, the sole seed bead manufacturer in Central Europe, becoming the private joint stock company *Ornela*, with divisions in Desná and Zásada.

Visits: Group visits are possible Mon.-Fri. 9am-12pm. Please phone in advance. The factory is in the heart of town, next to the former Riedel manor house (now a kindergarten).

Stores: In Desná, the two glass shops on the main street offer a limited selection of *Desná* glass. Open Mon.-Fri. 9am-5pm.

The former Riedel mansion, Desná. Photographer: Diane Foulds.

Photo: ČTK.

DUBÍ U TEPLIC

Avirunion, a.s. - Cristal Rudolfova Huť
Ruská 84
CZ-417 03 Dubí u Teplic
Tel. (0417) 3121
Fax   721 05

THE MONEY-SAVING technique of mechanically pressing molten glass into metal moulds was perfected in the United States in the 1820s. Dozens of Bohemian glassworks also employed the technique, but *Rudolfova Huť* was the only one that made a name for itself with pressed glass.

The original aim was to provide an inexpensive substitute for lead crystal. Some classic pressed models might be mistaken for hand-blown crystal.

Rudolfova Huť (Rudolf Hütte) was founded in 1884 as a sheet metal factory. Josef Inwald bought it in 1905 and converted it to glassmaking the following year. In the beginning the works blew household glass - vases, bottles, bell jars, lamps, and bowls - most of which was then painted and decorated. Later the works started producing glass that was manually pressed into moulds. Inwald also owned glassworks in Poděbrady, Prague, Vienna, and Budapest, but *Rudolfova Huť* was the feather in his cap. The success story came to an end after 1938, when Hitler annexed the Sudetenland.

After the war, all four Bohemian factories producing pressed glass were consolidated and placed under *Sklo Union* in Teplice. These were, in addition to *Rudolfova Huť, Libochovice, Rosice,* and *Heřmanova Huť.* The quality of *Rudolfova Huť*'s glass was always the highest among this group, and the sales figures proved it. During the 1950s, the state began replacing manual production with mechanization. Since that time, *Rudolfova Huť* has increasingly oriented itself

Photographer:
Pavel Frič.

towards low-cost, functional glass. Bottle making was automated in 1958, and the works began producing imprinted bottles for international soft-drink companies such as Coca-Cola, Pepsi, and Canada Dry. In 1978 *Rudolfova Hut'* was incorporated into *Obas Teplice*, later renamed *Obalunion Teplice*. In May 1992, part of the factory became an independent mould producer called *Formy*. *Rudolfova Hut'* is now part of *Avirunion*, a joint venture between *Obalunion* and Italy's *A.V.I.R. Finanzinaria*. *A.V.I.R. Milano* is one of the largest bottling companies in Italy, with more than half of the domestic market.

Since March 1993, *Rudolfova Hut'* has been selling its pressed household glass under the brand name *Cristal*. It still produces some of the elegant sets that won it acclaim in the 1930s, and has added some colorful new models. This is the company to turn to for cake platters, salad bowls, and serving dishes.

Visits: No factory tours are possible.

Stores: There is no factory store. In Dubí, *Ada Crystal Glass - Krušnohorská 5*.

Tel./Fax (0417) 721 04.
Open Mon.-Fri. 9am-12pm, 1pm-6pm, Sat. till 12pm.

HARRACHOV

N and S Bohemia Glassworks - Harrachov
(Sklárna N and S Bohemia - Harrachov)
CZ-512 46 Harrachov
Tel. (0432) 92 93 35
Fax   92 93 37
Telex   194617

T HERE is hardly a glassmaker in the Czech Republic who does not regard this small plant tucked in the foothills of the Krkonoše Mountains with a special reverence. Established in 1712 in Nový Svět (Neuwelt), it is the second oldest Bohemian works still operating. What sets it apart is the undiminished excellence of its crystal. There is a noble air about *Harrachov* glass; even its modern designs are marked by the grace of a past age. The tradition of exclusive elegance is partly due to the aristocratic origins of the house: This northernmost of Bohemian glass factories was founded on the estate of Count Alois Raimund von Harrach.

Some of the most famous Bohemian glassmakers worked here, and many pivotal styles were invented in *Harrachov* workshops. Milk glass, for example, a white glass that served as a good imitation of porcelain, was produced in large quantities starting in 1764.

In the 1820s, this was the only Bohemian works producing ruby glass colored with gold, or embedding ceramic cameos into cut glass. It was also the first glasshouse in Bohemia to manufacture cut lead crystal following its introduction by the English in the second half of the 18th century. At its workshops in Neuwelt, *Harrachov* employed some of the most skilled engravers of the day, including Dominik Bimann (1800-57), considered the greatest portraitist of the Biedermeier period. Throughout the 19th century, *Harrachov* and the now extinct *Adolfov* works near Vimperk rivaled each other as the region's premier producers. *Harrachov* was a pioneer in adopting the Art Nouveau, or *Jugendstil*, style. At its peak, colored floral designs applied to transparent glass were a characteristic feature.

Harrachov was nationalized in 1945, and incorporated into Crystalex in 1958. In July 1993, it became a private company once more. Every piece of glass is still made by hand, sometimes using hot-shaped techniques. *Harrachov* is probably the only glass factory left in the world that still cuts lead crystal on stone cutting wheels powered by a water turbine. A Baroque statue of St. Florian, the patron saint that protects against fires, stands guard over the furnace hall.

The new Harrachov emblem is a stylized dark blue and gold "H" over the date 1712.

Visits: Groups only. Advance booking is essential. Look for the smokestack, and don't miss the museum up the road (see "Museums" in Part Six).

Stores: There is a shop at the factory and another in the same building as the museum but entered separately.

In Prague, *Dana* - Národní třída 14 and Perlova 10, Prague 1. Open Mon.-Fri. 9am-7pm, Sat. till 6pm, Sun. 11am-6pm. Credit cards.
N & S Bohemia - Jugoslávská 25, Prague 2. Tel. (02) 25 95 74. Open Mon.-Fri. 10am-6pm, Sat. 9am-2pm.

Photo: Crystalex.

Photo: Zdenka Kalabisová and Antonín Krčmář.

HEŘMANOVA HUŤ

Union Heřmanova Huť, a.s.
CZ-330 24 Heřmanova Huť
 u Plzně
Tel. (019) 913 11 24
Fax   91 32 76
Telex   154320

HEŘMANOVA HUŤ is synonymous with machine-made pressed glass. This type of glass is usually valued more for its virtue of practicality than for beauty, yet *Heřmanova Huť* items are as attractive as they are utilitarian. They are made from a very clear, high-quality crystal, and the designs are more imaginative than what you'd normally expect from pressed glass. Low prices add to the appeal.

   The works, located a 30-minute drive northwest of Prague, produces vases, ice buckets, desert cups, ashtrays, and candlesticks, as well as the tall, slender kind of beer tumblers you find in German and Scandinavian beer halls.

   The factory is named after Baron Dietrich Hermann von Lindheim, who built an ironworks on the site in the mid-19th century. The ironworks closed in 1903, but two brothers named Stölzl moved in four years later and founded a glass company. They began with pharmaceutical glass, and introduced pressed glass within two years. *Heřmanova Hut's* heyday was 1927-29, when 740 workers put out a wide assortment of hand-decorated crystal. It experienced another boom in the 1930s despite the Great Depression, but World War II spelled the end of its prosperity. *Heřmanova Huť* was nationalized by the Czechoslovak government after the war and merged with other producers of pressed glass. Automatic bottle-making machines were installed in the Communist era, and production was almost 100% automated by 1971.

   Heřmanova Huť is now a subsidiary of *Sklo Union*, the industrial glass trust in Teplice. The focus is still on beer tumblers and household glass, although medicine bottles and small bottles with stoppers are also produced.

Visits: Visitors are welcome, but are asked to phone at least one week in advance.
Stores: There is a shop at the factory. Open Mon.-Fri. 8am-2pm.

JABLONEC NAD NISOU

Costume Jewelry Company
(Bižuterie, a.s.)
U přehrady
CZ-466 23 Jablonec nad Nisou
Tel. (0428) 512
Fax   121 35

THE SPECIALTY of *Bižuterie* is imitation jewelry, sumptuously woven into earrings, necklaces, tiaras, hair barrettes, belts, buttons, and numerous other types of accessories. *Bižuterie* makes the kind of jewelry that little girls dream of - dazzling in the Hollywood manner. With 1,400 employees, it is the largest producer of imitation jewelry in the world.

Bižuterie ("costume jewelry" in Czech) was once part of the gigantic state-run *Jablonecká bižuterie* trust. In 1990 it split off on its own and built a modern headquarters next to the lake in Jablonec nad Nisou. It cooperated with a variety of small jewelry and glass workshops, including the *Preciosa* enterprise, throughout the Communist period.

The word "rhinestone" comes from the French *caillou du Rhin* (stone of the Rhine), so called because they were originally made at Strasbourg, on the river Rhine. The invention of the rhinestone is credited to Josef Strasser, a Viennese jeweler. Intended to imitate diamonds, rhinestones are frequently referred to as "strass."

Bižuterie creates over 5,000 strass jewelry and button models each year, 80% of which are exported. The faceted rhinestones used are supplied primarily by *Preciosa* or the *Swarovski* company in Austria, while *Bižuterie* manufactures the metal parts and does the assembly.

The lion's share of *Bižuterie's* production was exported to the Soviet Union until about 1990. Shortly thereafter, the company redirected the bulk of its exports

to the United States, which remains its largest customer.

In 1992, *Bižuterie* started producing fragile glass Christmas tree ornaments, which are blown, painted, and decorated in a newly remodeled wing of its Jablonec complex. It has also begun minting Czech coins.

The *Bižuterie* logo is the letter "B" topped with a gold crown.

Visits: No factory tours are possible.

Stores: *Bižuterie* rhinestone jewelry is sold in costume jewelry stores throughout the Czech Republic.

In Jablonec nad Nisou, *Bohemia Strass* - Across from the town hall on Náměstí Míru. Open Mon.-Fri. 9am-6pm, Sat. till 12pm.

In Prague, *Royal* - The best address for costume jewelry. Na příkopě 12, Prague 1. Tel. (02) 24 21 05 52. Open Mon.-Sat. 9am-7pm, Sun. 10am-7pm. Traveler's checks, credit cards.

JABLONEC NAD NISOU
Preciosa, Ltd.
Opletalova 17
CZ-466 67 Jablonec nad Nisou
Tel. (0428) 41 51 11
Fax   282 90
Telex   184536

THERE are only two major producers that know the secret of cutting diamond-like glass stones using computer-controlled machines. One is *Swarovski* in Austria, and the other is *Preciosa*.

Preciosa stones are so clear and precision-cut that they flash the color spectrum when held up to the light. The most important is the *chaton*, which resembles a small diamond and is used in jewelry. *Preciosa* also makes multiple-faceted round beads and "fancy stones," which are generally rectangular or oval like the gems in rings. On the underside of chatons and fancy stones is a foil, i.e. a silver coating that adds brilliance to the stone's glitter.

Preciosa is unique not only on account of the superb cut of its

stones but also because it produces crystal chandelier pendants that contain no lead. In addition to chandeliers, its finished products include crystal figurines and, to a lesser extent, costume jewelry of faceted crystal beads. All are exported worldwide through the company's own sales channels, which include offices in New York and Madrid.

At its headquarters in Jablonec nad Nisou, *Preciosa* continues the northern Bohemian tradition of glass stone cutting which goes back to the early 18th century. From 1867 on, Jablonec (Gablonz in German) witnessed an astonishing boom in local costume jewelry production. To keep standards high, a special jewelry-making school was founded in 1880 (it still exists today). Manual stone cutting was an arduous business before electric cutting machines became standard equipment following World War I. Not only did they simplify the work but they also improved the quality of the stones.

The area's glass-cutting workshops were nationalized in 1948, and seven were merged to form *Preciosa*. In 1958 the state established a trust employing 27,000 which was eventually named Jablonecká bižuterie. It comprised all glass-making and costume jewelry enterprises in and around Jablonec, including *Preciosa.* While in this trust, *Preciosa* became in the early sixties the world's first producer of a fully machine-cut and polished octagonal pendant known as a "head," which gave rise to a whole new generation of *Preciosa* chandeliers.

Preciosa has come a long way since the fifties, and is now one of the strongest and most technically advanced of Czech glass producers. After the 1989 revolution, it became a private, independent company, fulfilling a long-held dream of many of its employees.

Visits: No factory tours are possible.

Stores: In Jablonec, *Preciosa* - Podhorská 20. Tel. (0428) 870 58. Open Mon.-Fri. 8am-4pm.

In Prague, *Světlo-Lux* - Národní třída 23, Prague 1.
Tel. (02) 72 93 72. Open Mon.-Fri. 9am-7pm, Sat. 10am-5pm.
Royal - Na příkopě 12, Prague 1. Tel. (02) 2421 05 52. Open Mon.-Sat. 9am-7pm, Sun. 10am-7pm. Traveler's checks.

In Brno, *Glass Market* - Orlí 9. Tel. (05) 246 47. Open Mon.-Fri. 9am-6pm, Sat. till 1pm.

In Karlovy Vary, *Madonna* - Lázeňská 7/23. Tel. (017) 222 07. Open daily 9:30am-6pm.

Photographer:
Ondřej Kavan.

JABLONEC NAD NISOU

Glass Costume Jewelry
(Skleněná bižuterie, a.s., Alšovice)
Smetanova 19
CZ-466 01 Jablonec nad Nisou
Tel. (0428) 245 44,
          204 47
Fax   245 44

SKLENĚNÁ BIŽUTERIE is the Czech Republic's largest producer of jewelry made from pressed-glass beads. It works with a cottage industry of bead makers whose output comes in every imaginable size, shape, and design. The company warehouse is a treasure trove of beads, which are loaded into sacks so heavy that only forklifts can move them around. Even the cracks in the floor are studded with brilliant dots of color.

Beads have been produced in this region for centuries, largely by craftsmen working at home. Merchants would go around at regular intervals and buy the finished product from each one. After World War I, bead makers were employed in small workshops. By 1936, 100,000 local inhabitants were employed in 1,100 such workshops.

When the curtain came down on private enterprise after World War II, any workshops that weren't nationalized were closed. For a while bead production ceased altogether. Then in the 1950s, state enterprises were formed and the manufacturing of costume jewelry was gradually resumed. The main enterprise was the *Železnobrodské sklo* works, which consolidated about one hundred small producers under its pressed-bead division in Alšovice near Jablonec nad Nisou. This factory was the forerunner of today's *Skleněná bižuterie.*

After the Velvet Revolution, *Skleněná bižuterie* split off from *Železnobrodské sklo* and became an independent joint-stock company. It now employs about 600, half of them artisans working at home. One-third of its production is devoted to costume jewelry - fashion necklaces, hippie love beads, rosaries, worry-beads, sophisticated earrings, pins, and belts, all in a range of colors. The rest of its production is devoted to beads and semifinished products, as well as lighting fixtures with delicate gold and glass filaments rather than the standard crystal chandelier trimmings. A whopping 80% of *Skleněná bižuterie*'s output is exported.

Photo: *Skleněná bižuterie.*

Visits: No factory tours are possible.

Stores: There is no factory store. In Prague, *Royal* - Na příkopě 12, Prague 1. Tel. (02) 24 21 05 52. Mon.-Sat. 9am-7pm, Sun. 10am- 7pm. Traveler's checks. *Jafa* - Maiselova 15, Prague 1. Tel. (02) 231 00 40. Open daily 9am-7pm. Credit cards, shipping service, currency exchange office.

JANOV NAD NISOU

Janov Glassworks
(Sklárna Janov)
CZ-468 11 Janov nad Nisou
Tel. (0428) 952 41, 953 94,
               952 42
Fax   952 50

THE JANOV works is one of the few Czech glass factories where up to twelve different colors can be melted in one furnace simultaneously. Usually a furnace melts only a few at a time, since each color requires a different temperature and the vapors from one may interfere with and ruin the next. *Janov* uses special equipment to isolate each color, turning out vases or perfume bottles in red, lavender, blue, aqua, green, white, orange, and yellow on any given day.

The works was built in 1912 by Johann Schorm, when the thriving costume jewelry industry in nearby Gablonz (Jablonec nad Nisou) needed alternative sources of glass raw materials. *Janov* initially made colorful glass bangles destined for India, but the outbreak of World War I disrupted their export and Schorm's company had no choice but to shut down until after the war. Bracelet exports resumed but never achieved their prewar volume. To compensate, the factory took up the production of colored glass rods, which it supplied to the jewelry and button manufacturers in the Jablonec area.

Since its nationalization after World War II, *Janov* has concentrated on pressed glass and glass produced through a combination of pressing and blowing techniques. Its 130 employees currently make over 120 small articles in a palette of different colors - ashtrays, candleholders, candy dishes, paperweights, salt shakers, perfume bottles, and much more. Some 90% is exported. The miniature perfume bottles are decorated with glass jewels, cameos, and metal filigree by *Bižuterie* in Jablonec.

Among Janov's most interesting items is its unique line of glass boxes. They can be square, round, or oval, in violet, blue, white, and malachite (jade glass). Pressed into the lids are roses, birds, floral patterns, and romantic nudes.

Visits: Visitors are welcome Mon.-Fri. 7am-12pm.
Groups are asked to phone in advance.

Stores: There is a shop at the factory. Open Mon.-Fri. 8am-1pm.

JOSEFODOL

Caesar Crystal s. r. o.
CZ-582 91 Josefodol u Světlé nad
 Sázavou
Tel. (0451) 522 01

THE JOSEFODOL works, which
produces cut lead crystal and
colorful layered, or "cased"
crystal, had been a subsidiary of
the *Sklo Bohemia* corporation in
neighboring Světlá nad Sázavou
since that works was established
in 1967. *Josefodol* is a small factory on a country road in the
middle of a forest, with a mere
150 employees. Yet *Josefodol* is
where the *Sklo Bohemia* cut glass
empire really started.

When *Josefodol* was founded in
1782, it made brass accessories.
Later it was converted into a
paper mill, which eventually
closed down. The premises were
bought by the Viennese glass
merchant Josef Schreiber, who
owned 11 other glassworks in
Bohemia and Slovakia, including
Lednické Rovne, and he put in a
glass-cutting workshop, which
began production in 1861. At first
Schreiber purchased blanks, or
undecorated glass, for the

Photographer:
Miroslav
Vojtěchovský.

workshop to decorate. But to save on transportation costs, he decided to build his own furnaces on the factory grounds. *Josefodol* manufactured glass intended for cutting and decorating, but it also produced lighting fixtures and oil lamps. The works later became known for its colored glass, ruby and purple being especially popular.

After the Schreiber era, *Josefodol* passed through several owners. The last were the brothers Čeněk and František Císař, who also owned *Tasice* and a few cutting workshops nearby. The Communist authorities confiscated *Josefodol* from the Císař family in 1948, and for several years the works was restricted to making technical and optical glass. Gradually it was able to return to the lavishly cut lead crystal for which it had been famous. At present, *Sklo Bohemia* and *Josefodol* are virtually the only Czech works producing cased 24% lead cut crystal in a palette that includes vivid crimson, mint green, royal blue, purple, and black.

Josefodol also puts out the occasional designer piece. Zdeněk Kunst and Josef Švarc are two of the glass artists who have designed for the works. *Josefodol* split off from *Sklo Bohemia* and became a private company in 1993.

Visits: Visitors are welcome, but are asked to phone in advance. From the top end of the main square in Světlá nad Sázavou, turn left and drive out of town until you see a sign for Josefodol. Turn right onto a road that climbs up the hill and into a forest. Make a left at the stop sign. The works is a short distance away.

Stores: There is no store at the factory, but *Josefodol* glass is carried in *Sklo Bohemia* shops (see under *Světlá nad Sázavou.*)

In Prague, *Cristallino* - Celetná 12, Prague 1. Tel. (02) 22 83 66. Open daily 9am-8pm.

KAMENICKÝ ŠENOV

Bratři Jílkové, s. r. o.
ul. Osvobození 512
CZ-471 14 Kamenický Šenov
Tel. (0424) 926 19
Fax   925 35

KAMENICKÝ ŠENOV is a rough Czech translation of the town's original German name, Steinschönau, which means "beautiful stone." For centuries local craftsmen cut and polished gemstones - and later glass gemstone imitations - and painted porcelain. The decorating tradition goes back further than in neighboring Nový Bor. In the 16th and 17th centuries, an artisan would spend the winter meticulously cutting and engraving a collection of beakers, mugs, decanters, and vases. Come spring, he would pack them in carts which he then pushed on foot to markets in Paris, Amsterdam, or Berlin. The journey took about a month, and on the way back he would load up with enough undecorated glass to last him through the following winter.

Companies were gradually formed to export the glass by horse and carriage, and branch offices were opened abroad. At one point there were six subsidiaries of Steinschönau firms in Constantinople, set up to do business with wealthy buyers from Arab kingdoms.

The timber house next to the church in the town center was where the first school of glass decorating in the world was founded in 1856. It is now a private residence. The school, however, still exists, housed in a larger building up the hill.

In 1771, 312 decorators were recorded as working in the town; by 1875, the number had grown to 1,000. So much did Steinschönau concentrate on decorating that it frequently ran out of glass. Until glass-making furnaces were built, the glass had to be transported, at considerable cost, from other parts of the country. The need for locally produced glass was met first by the *Adolf Rückl* works, founded in 1886. The *Jílek* family opened a factory in the valley in 1905. In 1925 the *František Vetter* works was the last to be established. The *Rückl* works later became *Severosklo*, a producer of technical glass, the *Jílek* works was absorbed by the *Crystalex* group, and the site of the *Vetter* works is occupied by a *Crystalex* warehouse.

Currently, the former *Jílek* works is the only factory left in Kamenický Šenov that both blows and decorates luxury household glass, although two other companies are planning to do the same in 1994. The most popular items are layered vases gilded in the "paneled" design and painted with tiny golden leaves

(lištovačka). Arab water pipes are also produced. The works was purchased in 1993 by an investment group including descendants of the Jílek family.

Visits: Visitors are welcome, but are asked to phone in advance.

Stores: *Kamenický Šenov* glass is sold in the shop in the local Glass Museum (see "Museums" in Part Six), and in Crystalex stores in Nový Bor and Prague.

Photo: Crystalex

KAMENICKÝ ŠENOV

Chandeliers
(Lustry)
CZ-471 14 Kamenický Šenov
Tel. (0424) 927 21-9
Fax   927 39

THE LUSTRY company is one of the world's leading producers of luxury chandeliers. *Lustry* chandeliers hang in Milan's La Scala and the Royal Opera in Rome, in the Waldorf-Astoria Hotel in New York, at Versailles and the Hermitage, and in King Ibn Saud's residence in Riyad. Up to 3,000 different models are available, ranging from delicate, bejeweled wall lamps to massive, two-ton showpieces. Opulent versions adorn castles and palaces in Paris, Moscow, Madrid, Berlin, Bombay, Ottawa, Manila, and many other cities, as well as the parliaments in Ankara, Sofia, Teheran, and Ulan Bator. Probably the largest chandelier ever made at *Lustry* is the giant fixture in the Palace of Culture in the Kazakh capital of Alma-Ata: it is 16 meters (52 feet) long, has 936 150-watt bulbs, and weighs 7.5 tons!

Kamenický Šenov has been a chandelier-making center for more than two and a half centuries. Josef Palme opened the first store and workshop in 1724. Within three years, orders had come in from the likes of King Louis XV of France. In 1746, Austrian Empress Maria Theresa commissioned a chandelier for her palace. This became known as the "Maria Theresa" model.

As chandeliers increased in popularity, more companies opened up in the Steinschönau area, many by descendants of Josef Palme. Eliáš Palme's enterprise was the most famous throughout the latter half of the 19th century, winning prizes at exhibitions in Vienna, Paris and Philadelphia. Production halted during World War II, and in 1946, all chandelier companies were nationalized and placed under one roof. *Lustry* was founded at that time. At first it was known as *Spojené továrny na lustry (United Chandelier Works)*, then it was renamed *Lustry Kamenický Šenov*. A modern production hall was opened in the early 1970s.

Lustry has five main types of lighting fixtures: crystal-pendant chandeliers, enamel overlay chandeliers, the "Maria Theresa" model, ornate bronze fixtures, and simple hanging lamps.

Visits: No tours of the production hall are possible. Groups may sometimes visit the showroom if they call in advance.

To see *Lustry* chandeliers aglitter in Prague, spend an evening at the National Theater or the Estates Theatre.

Stores: In Kamenický Šenov - The company shop is opposite the local Glass Museum at Osvobození 770.
Tel. (0424) 923 95. Open Tues.-Fri. 8:30am-4:30pm, Sat. till 12pm.

In Nový Bor - Masarykova 42. Tel. (0424) 318 76. Open Mon.-Fri. 8am-5:30pm, Sat. till 12pm.

In Prague, *Lustry* - Jindřišská 17, Prague 1. Open Mon.-Fri. 9:30am-6:30pm, Sat. 8:30am-3pm. Credit cards. *Linie* - Jungmannova 27, Prague 1. Open Mon.-Fri. 10am-7pm, Sat. till 5pm, Sun. till 3pm. Credit cards.

Photo: *Lustry.*

KARLOVY VARY

Moser Co., Ltd.
Kpt. Jaroše 19,
CZ-360 06 Karlovy Vary
Tel. (017) 416 123-5
Fax   436 19
Telex   156203

MOSER is the Rolls Royce of Bohemian glass; it is what world leaders give and receive as gifts. The company literature proudly refers to it as "the glass of kings," and it's not just hype. Czech President Václav Havel presented Emperor Akihiti of Japan with an engraved *Moser* fruit bowl. In the more distant past, patrons have included Austrian Emperor Franz Josef I, King Victor Emmanuel III of Italy, Pope Pius XI, the Shah of Iran, Ethiopian Emperor Haile Selassie, King Faisal of Saudi Arabia, King Hussein of Jordan, Britain's Queen Elizabeth II, and dozens of other monarchs, maharajahs, princesses, presidents, and ambassadors.

Anything coming out of the *Moser* glassworks is as good as a collector's item. *Moser* may not make the most expensive crystal in the world - although a single wineglass might cost well over USD $100 - but few other producers can rival its pieces for sheer magnificence.

The history of the company is a classic rags-to-riches story. Ludwig Moser, a glass engraver from the spa town of Karlsbad (Karlovy Vary), started out as the owner of a glass shop and engraving business that steadily expanded for 16 years until 1873, by which time he had sales offices in the most important world trade centers. It took him another two decades to persuade the authorities to let him build his own furnaces, so that the quality

of the glass itself might be as superb as its decoration. If Ludwig lived by one principle, it was perfectionism.

When permission was finally granted in 1893, Ludwig was already 60, but he built his glassworks. He also devised a secret formula for manufacturing glass as hard as rock and as brilliant as lead crystal, without the use of lead. Ludwig died in 1916, leaving the business to his son Leo, who saw to it that quality improved still further. The family's influence in the company declined during the Great Depression, and Leo Moser was forced to sell out in 1938.

Though the company was nationalized after World War II, its products continued to be sold under the famous *Moser* trademark. In 1990 it became a joint-stock company once again.

Visits: A day trip to the lovely Karlovy Vary spa is a must for visitors to Prague who have time to get out of the capital. Try to schedule in a stop at the *Moser* factory store and museum. Open Mon.-Fri. 7:30am-4pm. Tel. (017) 416 166. Credit cards, shipping service.
The glassworks is off Rte. 6. Follow the signs for Cheb. You'll see the blue *Moser* factory sign on the left.

Stores: In Prague, *Moser* - With its recently renovated interior featuring mahogany paneling and stained-glass windows, this is the most elegant glass shop in all of Central Europe. Na příkopě 12, Prague 1. Tel. (02) 24 21 12 93. Open Mon.-Fri. 9am-7pm, Sat. till 4pm. Credit cards, shipping service.

In Karlovy Vary, *Moser* - Founded by Ludwig Moser in 1885, the shop is still on its original premises.

Stará louka 40.
Tel. (017) 244 69. Open Mon.-Fri.
9am-5pm. Credit cards, shipping
service.

In Bratislava, *Toreza* - Rybárská
brána 2. Tel. (07) 33 02 60. Open
Mon.-Fri. 9:30am-6pm, Sat. 9am-
1pm. Credit cards.

Photo: *Moser
Co., Ltd.*

KAROLINKA

*Crystalex -
Karolinka Glassworks*
(Crystalex -
Sklárna Karolinka)
CZ-756 05 Karolinka
Tel. (0657) 916 20-2
Fax   911 31
Telex   052471

KAROLINKA, like *Květná* and
Vrbno, is a Moravian works
noted for its pastel-colored
contemporary glassware with artistic touches. *Karolinka* also specializes in classic stemware shapes
etched with intricate filigree patterns.

The works was founded by the Reich family in 1861 to make beer and water glasses. Later bottles, jars, and other articles were added to its production line. Its capacity slowly expanded, and new glassworkers brought in

was the biggest of the three. In the 1960s, all became part of *Crystalex* in Nový Bor.

Designer Antonín Švec and more recently Jana Matoušková and Alena Holišová have been crucial assets to *Karolinka*, reinforcing the

decorative skills from outside, especially etching. By the turn of the century, Reich had developed a world reputation for etched glassware under the trademark "R". Success gave way to the lean years of the 1930s, when the factory teetered on the brink of bankruptcy.

Production was halted during World War II, but resumed in 1945, continuing throughout the nationalization wave and the difficult period of restructuring that followed. In 1950, *Karolinka* was merged with *Květná*, and eleven years later, *Vrbno* was added to the collective, known as the *Moravian Glassworks*. *Karolinka*

works' reputation for simple lines and tasteful decoration. *Karolinka* has an assembly line which accounts for about half of its production, but also continues to put out delicate, thin-walled classics made by hand with exquisite filigree etching.

Visits: The factory is in the center of the town of Karolinka, which is in Moravia's Beskydy hills about a 15-minute drive from Vsetín. Be sure to phone in advance. While in the neighborhood, drop in at the open-air museum in Rožnov pod Radhoštěm to experience a perfect recreation of Moravian village life in the 19th century.

Stores: There is a shop at the factory. Open Mon.Fri. 8:30am-3:30pm.

In addition to the following stores, Karolinka glass is sold in *Crystalex* shops throughout the Czech Republic.

In Prague, *Bohemia Crystal* - Karlova 25 and Karlova 22, Prague 1.
Open daily 10am-7pm.

In Karlovy Vary, *Cristallicka* - Stará louka 63. Open daily 10am-6pm.

KATARÍNSKA HUTA (Slovakia)

Poltár Glassworks Co., Ltd., Katherine Works
(Sklárne Poltár, a.s., závod Katarínska Huta)
SK-985 23 Katarínska Huta
Tel. (0863) 9691 04

The stylistic focus was on layered glass in delicate colors, and goblets decorated with matte finishes and pantograph etchings.

Production was interrupted by World War I, but the 1920s

Photographer: Miroslav Vojtěchovský.

KATARÍNSKA HUTA was one of several glassworks established in Slovakia in the mid-19th century, and the second oldest still operating today. Štefan and Gejza Kuchynka opened it in 1841 to produce crystal suitable for cutting, as well as standard household glass. The brothers also owned the glassworks in Málinec.

But it wasn't until Jan Kozsuch took it over in 1849 that *Katarínska Huta* began to flourish. He invested in new buildings and equipment at a time when few glassworks were expanding in central Slovakia. On Kozsuch's death in 1863, the company passed to his widow, Karolina. Quality improved and sales rose. *Katarínska Huta* won several prizes at international fairs between 1876-79 for its cut and layered glass in subtle colors. Karolina died in 1901, and her son-in-law, Zoltán Solty Eleöd, took over the management. In 1903, a fire virtually leveled the factory. When it was rebuilt, rooms for etching, painting, and cutting were added on, making *Katarínska Huta* the most modern glassworks of its time in Slovakia.

SLOVAKIA
GLASS

1 8 3 6

brought recovery and *Katarínska Huta* experienced the biggest export sales in its history. It was nationalized after World War II and became the administrative center of the *Stredoslovenské sklárne* (Central Slovak Glassworks) corporation, which included *Málinec* and *Zlatno*. When *Poltár* was set up in 1971, the headquarters was transferred there.

Although privatization is on the horizon, *Katarínska Huta* remains for now part of the *Poltár Glassworks Co., Ltd.*, which also oversees production at *Zlatno* and *Málinec*.

The factory currently manufactures contemporary drinking sets with creative touches, as well as machine-made tumblers.

Katarínska Huta's trademark is a blue clover on a white background above the initials "KH".

Visits: Visitors are welcome but are asked to phone in advance. Stores: There is no factory store. *Katarínska Huta* glass is sold at the shop at the main works in Poltár. Open Mon.-Fri. 6:30am-2:30pm.

In Bratislava, *Michel-Glascentrum* - Obchodná 44.

Tel. (07) 33 49 73.

Open Mon.-Fri. 9am-6pm, Sat. till 4pm.

In Prague, selected *Katarínska Huta* items can be found in the *Kotva* department store. Náměstí Republiky 1, Prague 1.

Tel. (02) 24 80 11 11. Open Mon.-Fri. 8am-7pm, Thurs. till 8pm, Sat. till 4pm. Credit cards.

KOŠŤANY

Košťany Glassworks and Pot Manufacturer
(Košťanské Sklárny a pánvárny, a.s.)
CZ-417 23 Košťany
Tel. (0417) 263 51
Fax   250 67

THE TOWN of Košťany (Kosten) was once renowned for the Art Nouveau glass produced at the *Elisabeth* works. Times changed, however, and many of the glassworks in and around Teplice went under after World War I. Today those that survived are producing industrial or utilitarian glass.

In addition to contemporary glass lamps, the *Košťany* glassworks makes ceramic pots in which glass batch (molten glass) is melted inside the furnace. It is currently the monopoly supplier of these pots to glassworks throughout the former Czechoslovakia, and also exports them to Austria, Germany, Switzerland, and Sweden. The pots, which are one to two meters in circumference, are made of a special kind of clay which must be able to withstand extreme melting temperatures virtually 24 hours a day. They have a life span of six to eight weeks.

Until the latter half of the 1940s, the *Košťany* plant was known by the name of its founder, František Tomšík. Tomšík was a young glassblower working at *Rudolfova Huť* in nearby Dubí. In 1886 he pooled his savings with some coworkers and purchased a plot of land. It was cheap, as the soil was rocky. A glassworks went up but there was no space for a decorating workshop, so the glass had to be decorated directly at the furnace. With the help of glassblowers returning from working abroad, the Tomšík plant created a unique line of wineglasses and tableware, later adding ceiling lamps to its production program. After World War I, it produced colored glass, cased glass, and luxury objects with painted designs. This was the most successful period for the factory. It was nationalized after World War II and its focus diverted away from drinking sets.

Today, glass lamps make up 50% of *Košťany's* output. They have a contemporary look and come in subtle colors like smoke, blue, beige, and marble. In January 1993 the works was purchased by a private Czech company.

Visits: No tours are possible.
Stores: In Prague, *Glas Shop* - Jindřišská 29, Prague 1.
Tel. (02) 24 21 34 85. Open Mon.-Fri. 8am-6pm, Sat. 10am-4pm. Credit cards.
In Teplice, *Glas Shop* - 28. října 1.
Tel. (0417) 259 11.

Photo: *Košťanské sklárny a pánvárny, a.s.*

In Plzeň, *Lux Glas Shop* - Dřevěná 9.
Tel. (019) 22 70 67.

KVĚTNÁ U UHERSKÉHO BRODU

Crystalex - Květná Glassworks (Crystalex - Moravské sklárny Květná)
CZ-687 66 Květná 171
Tel. (0633) 952 41, 952 42
Fax   953 43

K VĚTNÁ is the oldest glassworks in Moravia, and one of the most creative of all the Czech glasshouses. Its product lines include classic gilt-edged or engraved stemware and contemporary drinking sets with hot-shaped stems in unconventional shapes and pastel colors. These sculpted pieces have been a hit with foreign buyers. There are ultra-simple drinking sets with sophisticated black accents, and wineglasses splashed with abstract touches of color.

Květná can be traced back to 1794, when it was founded as the *Stranier Glashütte* by the aristocratic Lichtenstein family in the village of Strání. For the first 50 years of its existence it produced ordinary tableware and plate glass from common greenish-colored glass mass. The Viennese entrepreneur Emanuel Zahn purchased the factory in 1850, brought in experts to improve the raw materials used, and introduced the production of fine cut and engraved crystal, which was being successfully exported by the 1880s. Zahn's son, Emanuel, Jr., married a girl from the Goepfert glassmaking family, and in 1894 the works was renamed the *Zahn & Goepfert Glasfabrik Blumenbach*. Etched glass, painted glass, and other techniques appeared in 1896, and at the turn of the century, *Z & G* was appointed supplier to the imperial court in Vienna. With the exception of the World War I period and the Great Depression of the early 1930s, production continued straight through World War II.

Květná was nationalized in 1946 and merged with two other Moravian plants, *Vrbno pod Pradědem* and *Karolinka*. Within four years it had been reorganized again, later coming under the administration of *Crystalex*.

Since the 1950s, the two most important designers for *Květná* have been Ludvík Uher and František Brunovský, who favor thin-walled glass and tall, slender stems. The trumpet-shaped stem is a Brunovský trademark. *Květná* currently has 600 employees and continues to create elegant gilt stemware and artistic drinking sets, as well as decoratingmachine-made glass from the Crystalex-owned *Kombinát* in Nový Bor.

Visits: *Květná* in Strání is up against the Slovak border. If you're coming from Uherské Hradiště, drive southeast on Rte. 498. From Slovakia, drive northwest on Rte. 54 from the town of Nové Mesto nad Váhom. Phone a few days in ad-

Photo:
Lumír Rott.

vance to announce your visit.

Stores: The factory store is open Mon.-Fri. 8am-12pm, 1pm-3pm.

Closed the last two weeks in July.

Květná glass is sold in *Crystalex* stores throughout the Czech Republic.

LEDNICKÉ ROVNE (Slovakia)

Lednické Rovne Glassworks
(Spojené Sklárne Lednické Rovne)
SK-020 61 Lednické Rovne
Tel. (0825) 93 721
Fax   93 628
Telex   075361

THE LARGEST Slovak glass manufacturer, *Lednické Rovne*, makes spare, contemporary-looking drinking sets that are the closest thing to Scandinavian styles produced in the former Czechoslovakia, and as a result are extremely popular with foreign glass importers. About half the glassware is machine-made. Thanks to the broad appeal of its products and their low prices, *Lednické Rovne* can boast a production capacity that is often booked up solid.

Josef Schreiber founded the works in 1892 in the Lednica manor house. The owner of 11 other glassworks, he was considered the most important glass producer in Central Europe.

Lednické Rovne started out by producing flat glass. In 1893 it became the first works in the Austro-Hungarian Empire to make pressed glass that imitated cut crystal. By the following year it was selling blown glass under the trademark *Ronacrystal*. This was generally hotel stemware in simple, tasteful shapes, often designed by Viennese artists, with the logo of the establishment needle-etched, cut, or engraved.

The works came under new ownership in 1909. After World War I it added lampshades to its production line. It weathered the Depression

Photographer: Miroslav Vojtěchovský.

years fairly well. The factory was nationalized in 1946, and badly damaged in a fire a year later. When it was repaired, the decision was made to thoroughly modernize the works: automatic production lines were installed, and in 1958 it switched from the use of coal to natural gas.

In the 1960s, *Lednické Rovne* catered primarily to the domestic market. Steadily it began to boost its machine production capacity. In 1978-80, the plant helped develop equipment that employed lasers in automated glass decoration.

The major designers for *Lednické Rovne* have been Slovak artists Karol Hološko and Jaroslav Taraba, whose streamlined designs are still among the biggest sellers. The works, with its simple "LR" logo, is awaiting imminent privatization.

Visits: Visitors are welcome, but are asked to phone in advance.

Stores:

In Bratislava, *Franc Agentur* - Štefánikova 3. Tel. (07) 3321 30. Open Mon.-Fri. 10am-6pm, Sat. 8am-12pm.

In Prague - The company store, *Lednické Rovne*, is at Spálená 7, Prague 1. Tel. (02) 20 28 70. Open Mon.-Fri. 9:30am-6pm, Sat. 10am-1pm. *Poloma* - Francouzská 42, Prague 2. Tel. (02) 25 75 12. Open Mon.-Fri. 9am-12pm, 1pm-6pm, Sat. till 12pm.

LENORA

Šumava Glassworks
(Šumavské sklárny, a. s.)
CZ-384 42 Lenora
Tel. (0339) 988 33-35
Fax   988 68

A CENTURY AGO, *Eleonoren-hain,* now known as *Eleonora,* was one of the most highly regarded of all Bohemian glassworks. In our time, however, it served until recently as a mere backup producer to a larger factory, *Crystalex's Český Křišťál* at Chlum u Třeboně.

Founded in 1834 as part of the Meyr Glass Co., *Eleonora* is the oldest glassworks in southern Bohemia. Upon the death of Johann Meyr, it was taken over by Wilhelm Králík and Josef Taschek. The company was now known as *J. Meyr's Neffe,* and consistently won awards for the high artistic quality of its output. At first it focused on colored crystal, sometimes etched or iridized, along with a small amount of flat glass and glass for timepieces. After Králík died in 1877, the various glass factories he had owned were divided among his sons, with *Eleonoren-hain* going to Johann Králík.

Working in conjunction with *J.& L. Lobmeyr,* the works produced superb examples of colored glassware. It successfully experimented with *Jugendstil,* or Art Nouveau, designs. Periodic downturns were always followed by recovery, and the company prospered into the 1930s by exporting household glass in various price ranges within Europe and also to the Americas, despite the worldwide Depression.

World War II left *Eleonora* financially shattered, but the works persevered. It was the only one of three glassworks in southern Bohemia's Šumava region that was not bankrupt by the war's end. The other two, *Johann Loetz Witwe* in Klášterský Mlýn and *Adolf* in Vimperk, are documented in the museum in Kašperské Hory.

Eleonora was nationalized in 1946 and merged with the *Český Křišťál* works at Chlum u Třeboně, which became part of *Crystalex*. Over the years, its facilities have been renovated and modernized, although the creative colored glass for which the works was once renowned was largely abandoned. (The achievements of the past can be admired in a permanent exhibition in the local town hall; see "Museums" in Part Six.) *Eleonora*, working with its cutting workshop in Vimperk, currently makes cut lead crystal featuring colored painting and engraving.

Lenora, as it was called while part of Crystalex, was privatized in the autumn of 1993 under the name *Šumava Glassworks*.

Visits: Visitors are welcome, but are asked to phone in advance.

Drive south on Rte. 4 from Vimperk and follow the signs eastward towards Volary. Stores: *Lenora* sells its glass at its

Photo: Crystalex.

Lenora shop Mon.-Sat. 9am-3:30pm, and at four other locations in the region.

LIBOCHOVICE

Libs
CZ-411 17 Libochovice
Tel. (0419) 922 15
Fax   924 03

LIBS manufactures pressed glass in the form of bowls, plates, vases, and dessert sets. Some lines could be mistaken for cut lead crystal. Most of the factory's output was formerly sold domestically or within the Soviet bloc, although *Libs* now aims to expand its distribution westward.

The factory was founded in 1912 by two entrepreneurs who chose its site because of the close proximity to railway lines and coal deposits. Production was interrupted by World War I, but resumed after 1918. Some of the moulds for the most popular household pieces in the interwar years were imported from the United States. Rich colors were added to the production line and including Adolf Matura and Václav Zajíc, contributed their talents to *Libs* in the 1960s. Zajíc still designs for it today.

Libs was privatized early in 1993. Its current best-selling models are those reminiscent of 1920s

a decorating workshop was set up. Beer glasses and pressed-blown vases were among the company's most successful products.

After World War II the glassworks was nationalized and merged several times with other enterprises. Greater attention was paid to automation, and production capacity increased substantially. A number of innovative artists, styles, most with floral motifs or marked by the juxtaposition of matte and clear polished surfaces.

Visits: Visitors are welcome, but are asked to phone in advance. The factory is located northwest of Prague, off Rte. 55.

Stores: In Prague, *Labora* - Jungmannova 7, Prague 1. Tel. (02) 235 04 07. Open Mon.-Fri. 8am-12pm, 1pm-4:30pm.

LUČANY NAD NISOU
Jizera Glass
(Jizerské Sklo, a.s.)
CZ-468 71 Lučany nad Nisou
Tel. (0428) 823 41
Fax   823 68

JIZERSKÉ SKLO is one of two Czech suppliers of the colored glass rods used by craftsmen to make buttons, beads, figurines, and other small articles, and the only one that still makes them by hand. The tip of these long, thin bars are held over a flame, and the glob of hot glass that drips off is then wound, dabbed, or pressed into the desired shape or mould.

The rods, most of which are less than an inch in diameter, come in numerous colors, or even in a group of colors. They look something like a glass candy cane, or striped, translucent toothpaste squeezed out of the tube. The more colorfully complex rods are handmade. Two glassmakers take a large slab of molten glass and gently pull it and flex it from each end until it forms a long, thin strand, called "composition glass." It has the highest lead content found anywhere, about 48%, which gives it maximum pliability. The glass used in crafting miniature figurines has to be easy to manipulate.

In the first half of the 19th century, there were six works in the Jizera and Krkonoše Mountains manufacturing glass base materials and semifinished products for Jablonec nad Nisou's thriving glass and costume jewelry industries. The Lučany works was founded in 1914 by the Breit family, which oversaw the production of glass rods, rocaille, and beads. In 1946, the works was seized by the state and ultimately consolidated with other nearby glass producers into the monolithic *Jablonec Glassworks Corporation.*

Jizerské sklo, with its three production halls, has been a joint-stock company since 1990. Besides rods, it produces colorful hot-shaped vases and candlesticks and tiny perfume bottles. It is one of only a few Czech glassworks that makes salt and pepper sets and condiment servers, which are pressed in its *Josefův Důl* works and sold domestically.

Jizerské sklo's logo is "JIS" in a tear drop, which is what a particle of glass looks like under a microscope.

Visits: No tours are possible.

Stores: The company store is in the center of the village of Lučany. Tel. (0428) 822 04. Open Mon.-Fri. 8am-6pm, from June-Sept. till 12pm.

Photographer:
Diane Foulds.

Photographer:
Miroslav
Vojtěchovský.

POLTÁR
CRYSTAL

24% PbO

MÁLINEC (Slovakia)

Poltár Glassworks - Málinec Works
(Sklárne Poltár, a.s., závod
Málinec)
SK-985 26 Málinec
Tel. (0864) 3151
Fax   3156

MÁLINEC, one of five
glassworks operating in
Slovakia, manufactures
24% lead cut crystal in classic
designs, although historically it
has been a producer of colored
glass.

Throughout the 18th and 19th
centuries, the glass factories in
Slovakia competed with and at
times equaled their Bohemian
rivals in producing luxury crystal
destined for world markets. The
first half of the 19th century was a
period of intensive growth for
glass production in Slovakia. The
effects of the Napoleonic Wars
had been little felt and wages
were extremely low. Hungarian
aristocrats owned many of the factories, often hiring German
managers. The most significant
producers during this period were
clustered in central Slovakia,
where 30 works had operated continuously since the middle of the
17th century. Only half were still
in existence 200 years later. The
best known were in the towns of
Utekáč, Katarínska Huta, Zlatno,
and Málinec.

Málinec was founded in 1852 by
Štefan Kuchynka, who also owned
Katarínska Huta and the former
works at Sihla, and started out
producing plain soda-potash
household glass. Kuchynka and
his brother Gejza ran the works
until the latter's death, when it
was taken over by the Kollener
family, which managed it until
1930. Every kind of glass was
produced here, much of it
imitating successful styles coming
out of Bohemian decorating
workshops.

The factories in Slovakia had
complemented the glass produced
in Bohemia, and when companies
there lost orders, Slovakia fared
even worse. The development of
mass-production methods in the
United States meant tougher competition, and many of the factories
in Slovakia went out of business.
The situation deteriorated in the

20th century, but the four merged into the *Tatrasklo* complex. *Utekáč* changed its production line to technical glass and thermos-bottle liners. In the 1960s, *Tatrasklo* was disbanded and its three works were placed under the newly built *Poltár* factory. *Málinec* underwent a major reconstruction in 1987, during which the production of 24% lead crystal was introduced. The works ia still part of *Poltár* for the time being.

Visits: Visitors are welcome, but must phone in advance. Málinec is the northernmost of the four *Poltár* factories, located in a small village west of Detva.

Stores: *Málinec* glass is sold at the shop at the *Poltár* factory. Open Mon.-Fri. 6:30am-2:30pm.

MEDZILABORCE (Slovakia)

Lusk, a.s.
Dobrianského 1
SK-068 01 Medzilaborce
Tel. (0939) 212 64
Fax   219 31

LUSK is Slovakia's sole producer of luxury chandeliers and chandelier trimmings (pendants). Its original purpose was to provide a supplementary source of hand-cut chandelier trimmings for Czech producers in northern Bohemia. It began in 1970 as a branch of the Desná-based *Jablonec Glassworks Corporation*, which supplied the materials for the trimmings. The cutters were trained at Desná and Smržovka in the art of grinding crystal chandelier pendants on vertical wheels.

In 1985, *Lusk* set out to produce its own chandeliers and lighting fixtures. It is currently a private company employing 250. It produces about 100 models of chandeliers, table and bedside lamps, and wall-mounted fixtures, as well as pendants in over 300 faceted shapes: teardrops, crystals, orbs, and numerous dangling profiles. These pendants undergo a meticulous cutting process involving up to 10 grinding and polishing steps on sandstone or metal horizontal and vertical grinding wheels. An orb in the center of a chandelier may have as many as 120 facets, each of which has been ground and polished by hand on wooden or rubber wheels. A richly ornamented chandelier in a hotel or in an auditorium might contain as many as 3,000 of these sparkling pendants.

Since 1988, *Lusk* has expanded its line to include lamps and lamp shades with float, i.e. milk-like coatings, metal and glass lamp and chandelier components, etched and sand-blasted statuettes, miniature figurines crafted from faceted crystal pendants, and 24% lead crystal household glass, such as vases, bowls, and plates.

One of the company's advantages is its location near the borders with Poland and Ukraine, both longstanding customers.

Visits: Tours are possible if you phone in advance. Medzilaborce is in the northeastern corner of Slovakia on Rte. 559, only a few minutes from the Polish border. An unexpected addition to the local scene opened here in 1991 - a museum dedicated to the U.S. artist Andy Warhol, whose parents emigrated from the area.

NIŽBOR

Antonín Rückl and Sons, Ltd.
(Antonín Rückl a synové, sklárna
   Nižbor)
CZ-267 05 Nižbor
Tel. (0311) 935 86,
              932 02, 932 03
Fax   935 10
Telex   132432

THE RÜCKL family left Switzerland in the middle of the 18th century and settled in Bohemia, where they would spend the next 200 years producing glass. Seven generations of Rückls have been glassmakers; the ear-liest trained under Venetian masters. By the end of World War II, the family owned glassworks in *Nižbor, Včelnička,* and *Skalice u České Lípy.* When the state gave the order to nationalize the glass industry, the plants were seized and the Rückl signs torn off. But less than three years after the Velvet Revolution, the Rückl signs went back up. The *Nižbor* plant, which produces hand-cut lead crystal, is now under the management of Jiří Rückl, the great-grandson of the company's original founder.

Nižbor dates back to 1903. Its first products were soda-potash household glass and chandelier prisms. Lead crystal was put into production only in 1926. The factory closed down briefly during World War I, but has operated ever since. Between the wars, *Nižbor* produced glorious cut glass pieces in collaboration with some of Czechoslovakia's leading glass artists, such as the legendary Ludvika Smrčková, who was born the year the factory was founded and died in 1991.

After its nationalization, *Nižbor* was merged with three other lead crystal producers, *Poděbrady, Světlá nad Sázavou,* and *Antonínův Důl.* In later years, *Chlum u Třeboně* and *Lenora* were added on to expand output.

Since the return of the Rückls, Nižbor has become a proud, forward-thinking company. As a gesture to the past, it produced a series of romantic crystal perfume bottles with silky black fringed atomizers, reminiscent of the

1930s. More recently, it has introduced elegant crystal drinking sets that point to where this works is headed, namely towards innovation. Sprinkled among *Rückl's* classic items are some other departures, such as fanciful crystal cubes flushed with colored bubbles, animal figurines, elegant Art Deco replicas, and life-sized glass swords.

Rückl's trademark is a maroon sticker with a golden stork holding a stopper in its beak.

Visits: Visitors are welcome Mon.-Fri. 7am-1:30pm, if they phone in advance. Groups preferred. Get off the Prague-Plzeň highway at Exit 14. Follow the signs to Beroun, and bear right at the first traffic light. Nižbor is about 10 km away.

Stores: There is a shop at the factory. Open Mon.-Fri. 8am-2pm.

In Prague, *Crystal Galerie Rückl* - Dlouhá třída 19, Prague 1. Tel. 232 36 48. Open Mon.-Fri. 10am-7pm, Sat. till 2pm.

In Beroun, *Rückl & synové* - Husovo náměstí 28. Tel. (0311) 226. Open Mon.-Fri. 8am-6pm.

In Karlovy Vary, *Kvadrant* - Nová louka 9. Tel. (017) 227 59. Open Mon.-Sat. 10am-8pm, Sun. 11am-8pm.

In Chomutov, *Rückl & synové* - Příčná 28. Open Mon.-Fri. 9am-5pm.

In Český Krumlov, *Rückl & synové* - ul. Parkán 127. Tel. (0337) 2086. Open Mon.-Fri. 10am-6pm, Sat. till 1pm.

NOVÝ BOR

Crystalex Co., Ltd.
B. Egermanna 634
CZ-473 13 Nový Bor
Tel. (0424) 43 11 11, 43 22 09
Fax   322 50, 322 51
Telex   186282

WITH seven glassworks, two manufacturing plants, and close to 6,000 employees, the *Crystalex* corporation is the largest producer of household glass in the Czech and Slovak Republics. Its name is a composite of the words "crystal" and "export," which describe its main activities. In 1992, two-thirds of *Crystalex's* US $46 million turnover was exported to over 100 countries. Everything from ultra-modern glassware to historical replicas is produced under the *Crystalex* label, making it the most diverse of Czech glass companies.

Since 1989, *Egermann-Exbor,*

Chřibská, Harrachov, and *Lenora* have left the *Crystalex* fold and undergone privatization. The *Kamenický Šenov* plant followed suit at the end of 1993. The remaining seven are staying within *Crystalex* for the time being. They include the factories at *Chlum u Třeboně, Rosice, Květná, Vrbno,* and *Karolinka,* the *Zahn* works, and *Crystalex's* largest producer, the *Kombinát* in Nový Bor.

The *Crystalex* corporation was formed in 1973 from what had been known previously as *Borské sklo.* Apart from overseeing its member glassworks, it also manufactures its own packaging and runs a research wing that develops glassmaking machines and equipment.

Crystalex has been an active supporter of studio glass since the early 1980s, organizing and sponsoring four international *Interglass Symposia* (in 1982, 1985, 1988, and 1991). Established glass artists from all over the world are invited to use the *Kombinát's* production hall in an international "show and tell" that has yielded some remark-

Stores: *Crystalex* operates a network of excellent stores throughout the Czech Republic. In Prague, *Crystalex* - One of the best in the chain, especially for classic glassware. Malé náměstí 6, Prague 1. Tel. (02) 24 22 84 59.

Photo: *Crystalex.*

able avant-garde creations. Many of these works can be admired at Lemberk Castle near Nový Bor, where *Crystalex* has set up a permanent display of glass sculpture (see "Museums" in Part Six). Another place to see them is the spacious *Crystalex* sample showroom in Nový Bor. The next Symposium is tentatively planned for October 1994.

Visits: See the listings for the individual factories.

Open daily 9am-6pm.

Crystalex - Glass with more contemporary flair. Karlovo náměstí 6, Prague 2. Tel. (02) 29 12 60. Open Mon.-Fri. 9am-6pm, Sat. till 1pm.

In Nový Bor, *Crystalex*-Náměstí míru 100. Tel. (0424) 34 223. Open Mon.-Fri. 8am-5pm.

In Mariánské Lázně, *Crystalex*-Kolonáda. Tel. (0165) 2966. Open Wed.-Sun. 9am-5pm.

NOVÝ BOR

Crystalex - Kombinát
B. Egermanna 634
CZ-473 13 Nový Bor
Tel. (0424) 43 11 11, 43 22 30
Fax   338 46, 322 50, 322 51

THE KOMBINÁT is the largest household glass manufacturer in the Czech and Slovak Republics. Its six-furnace hall was built in 1967, and a state-of-the-art automated production line was installed in the early 1970s. Three others have been added since. Over two-thirds of glass production in the *Kombinát* is now done by machines, which can churn out up to 3,000 tulip-shaped wineglasses an hour. The stems are pressed and then whisked around to a device that holds them upright while a glob of molten glass is deposited on top to form the bowl.

The factory is impressive in terms of sheer size alone. In room after room of furnaces, glassblowers are making everything from the standard hourglass-shaped vase to avant-garde designs in mauve and turquoise.

Next door are the cutting and decorating studios, where the glass is meticulously hand-painted or carved on a vertically-spinning wheel. Some of the best-known glass types produced at the *Kombinát* include the classic high enamel, with its broad gold surfaces and painstaking flower-petal applications, enamel overlay glass with gilded and floral decoration, and contemporary painted vase and stemware design.

The impact of two designers in particular has been felt at the *Kombinát* over the past 20 years: Pavel Hlava and Jiří Šuhájek, both established studio artists. Hlava designed numerous award-winning machine-made stemware sets, and Šuhájek's influence can be seen in hot-shaped bowls, vases, and tumblers. The works has also benefited from the creative talents of artists Eva Švestková, Pavel

Photo: *Crystale*

112

Homolka, and Jaroslav Vymazal, all pupils of Stanislav Libenský, as well as the *Kombinát's* own design team, headed by Věra Libenská.

Visits: Visitors are asked to phone two weeks in advance to book a tour.

Stores: There is a shop at the factory. Look for the sign. Open Mon.-Fri. 9am-1pm, 1:30pm-3:30pm.

For a listing of retail outlets, see page 111.

NOVÝ BOR

Crystalex - Zahn Works
CZ-473 13 Nový Bor
Tel. (0424) 313 10, 332 42
Fax   320 19

THE ZAHN WORKS produces glass styles that are virtually unique in the Czech and Slovak Republics. These include cut lead crystal in pastel colors or painted with floral patterns and gold, and high enamel on a solid black background, known as the "Black Cat." The works, which has returned to its old name after more than 40 years, continues one of Nový Bor's oldest traditions: decorating glass in a combination of styles such as cutting, engraving, painting, sandblasting, and gilding. It is one of the few glassworks still producing lead crystal pieces that are both engraved and cut.

The factory was founded in 1895 by Johann Zahn, who originally intended it to be a cutting workshop. It was expanded to include a glassblowing hall and decorating workshops, concentrating primarily on classic cut lead crystal. In the interwar period, scores of skilled cottage workers were employed as back-up cutters and engravers, just to keep pace with demand.

Zahn was nationalized in 1948, and later incorporated into *Crystalex*. In the 1960s it developed the painting styles which it has retained until today, with the help of chief designer Zdeněk Němeček and more recently, Marta Macelová. Around 250 decorators work in a building on the outskirts of Nový Bor, acquired by *Zahn* in the 1920s. The crystal decorated in the workshop is blown about three miles (five km) away in the village of Prácheň near Kamenický Šenov.

The *Zahn* decorating workshop is on the edge of town across from a beautiful garden cemetery where some of Nový Bor's historical glassmaking families from the 19th century are buried.

Visits: Visitors are asked to phone in advance to arrange a tour.

Stores: There is a small shop at the *Prácheň glassblowing plant. Tel. (0424) 926 38. Open Mon.-Fri. 8am-12pm.*

Zahn glass is sold in *Crystalex* shops throughout the Czech Republic.

In Prague, *Crystalex* - Malé náměstí 6,

Prague 1. Tel. (02) 22 18 51. Open daily, 9am-7pm.

NOVÝ BOR

Egermann-Exbor
Dvořákova 306
CZ-473 01 Nový Bor
Tel. (0424) 314 03, 335 71
Fax   328 11

EGERMANN-EXBOR was so renowned before World War II that, like *Moser*, it couldn't be collectivized into anonymity under the postwar Czechoslovak state. It is probably most famous for the cherry-red stain which its founder, Friedrich Egermann (1777-1864), invented in 1832. But Egermann, a genius when it came to decorative techniques, made many more discoveries.

He started his career as a glass painter in *Chřibská*, then moved to the Meissen porcelain factory in Germany to study production techniques. Legend has it that he passed himself off as a deaf-mute to gain access to the painting workshops, where he learned Meissen's secrets of color preparation. Egermann was already an accomplished painter and successful entrepreneur by the time he returned to Bohemia. After establishing workshops in Nový Bor (known at the time by its German name, Haida) and nearby Polevsko, he set about making history. In 1816, he reinvented a bright yellow stain that had been used on 14th-century glass. He also worked on opaline glass and ventured upon an opaque variety called agate. At Prague exhibitions in 1828, 1829, and 1831, he displayed "lithyaline" glass that resembled semiprecious stones.

His inventions were admired and imitated all over the world. Although he attempted to patent his red stain, burglars broke into his workshop and stole the secret formula. Before long, red-stained glass began appearing in France and later in the United States.

Egermann's vision has endured. Despite nationalization and even-

Photographers:
Zdenka
Kalabisová and
Antonín Krčmá[r]

tual incorporation into the *Crystalex* corporation, *Egermann-Exbor* has never stopped creating new ideas. One of the marvels of this company is the sheer range of styles it produces: from Baroque-style engraved glass to geometric modernism and everything in between, including high enamel, glass with detailed landscapes, paperweights, modern designer stemware, and glass flowers. Since early 1993, it is once again a private company. Lately it has been active in the field of art glass, cooperating with studio artists like René Roubíček.

Visits: Visitors are welcome, but are asked to phone in advance.

Glassblowing is done at Nemocniční 339, referred to as the Hantych or Flora building, and decorating at Dvořákova 306.

Stores: In Prague, *Egermann-Exbor* - Na příkopě 13, Prague 1. Tel. (02) 22 00 95. Open daily 9am-7pm. Credit cards. Národní třída 17, *Egermann-Exbor* - Prague 1. Tel. (02) 243 02. Open daily 9am-7pm. Credit cards.

In Karlovy Vary, *Egermann-Exbor* - Stará louka 50. Tel. (017) 8632. Open daily 9am-7pm. Credit cards.

In Mariánské Lázně, *Egermann-Exbor* - Kolonáda 143. Tel. (0165) 5864. Open daily 9am-7pm. Credit cards.

NOVÝ BYDŽOV

Bydžov Glassworks
(Sklárny Bydžov)
CZ-504 11 Nový Bydžov
Tel. (0448) 234 93
Fax   233 97
Telex   194433

THE NOVÝ BYDŽOV works is one of six producing chandeliers in the Czech Republic. Its niche lies in smaller models intended for apartments or family houses. It also makes faceted chandelier trimmings in a variety of colors, which is a rarity in this type of fixture. The colors currently offered are topaz, deep blue, emerald, and rose.

Nový Bydžov opened in 1964 in the hall of what had been a textile factory. Until 1991 it was one of seven plants under the umbrella of the *Desná* concern, known then as the *Jablonec Glassworks* (*Jablonecké sklárny*). At first *Nový Bydžov* concentrated on cutting facets into pressed trimmings, which other plants would then use

in assembling luxury chandeliers. In 1970 it began producing whole chandeliers, half of which were exported to various parts of the Soviet Union. Small chandeliers were a popular item not only in Soviet government offices and assembly halls but also in subway stations, museums, and even grocery stores.

With the collapse of the Soviet market in 1990, the *Nový Bydžov* works shifted its attention to Poland, Germany, Sweden, Spain, and other markets. A good deal of its exports are made up of trimmings alone, 90% of which are hand-cut and polished from raw materials supplied by *Desná*. It also provides finished trimmings for the *Lustry* company in Kamenický Šenov, the country's largest chandelier producer. In 1985 *Nový Bydžov* started fashioning figurines from its chandelier trimmings in what soon became yet another export item. The *Jablonecké sklárny* conglomerate split up in 1991, and two years later, *Nový Bydžov* became a private joint-stock company.

Visits: No factory tours are possible.

Stores: Fifty chandelier models are available for sale in the sample room. The works is open Mon.-Fri. 6am-2:30pm. It's advisable to phone in advance.

In Prague, *Luna* - Na příkopě 16, Prague 1. Tel. 22 18 39. Open Mon.-Fri. 9am-7pm, till 4pm. *Kotva* - Naměstí Republiky 8, Prague 1. Tel. (02) 286 14 08. Open Mon.-Fri. 8am-7pm, Thurs. till 8pm, Sat. till 4pm. *R & B* - U Obecního domu 2, Prague 1. Open Mon.-Sat. 10am-6pm. Credit cards.

PODĚBRADY

Bohemia Glassworks
(Sklárny Bohemia, a.s.)
Naměstí T. G. Masaryka 1130
CZ-290 34 Poděbrady

Tel. (0324) 611 11, 62 111
Fax   24 18, 23 20

Photographers:
Zdenka
Kalabisová and
Antonín Krčmář

THIS IS one of the largest Czech producers of classically cut, 24% lead crystal. Its sparkling creations come in every conceivable form, from fragile perfume bottles and picture frames to opulent waist-high vases cut in a dazzling mosaic of swirls, grids, and patterns. The glass-encased showroom looks like the proverbial ice palace.

Until 1989, *Poděbrady* was lumped together with the country's other major cut glass producers - *Nižbor, Dobronín, Antonínův Důl,* and *Světlá nad Sázavou* - under the copyrighted trademark "Bohemia." After 1989, this conglomerate split up, although the *Dobronín* and *Antonínův Důl* plants did not go independent until 1993. *Poděbrady* and *Světlá nad Sázavou* continue to use the name "Bohemia," and still produce almost identical lines of crystal.

Founded in 1876, *Inwald,* as the factory was then called, originally concentrated on painted soda potash glass. Between the world wars it switched to lead glass, which the British had popularized on Western markets. Together with its affiliated works, *Poděbrady* today employs about 900, who work in any of the company's five glass-cutting halls. The glassworks also wholesales large quantities of semifinished glass, or blanks, to private glass cutters.

The giveaway of a *Poděbrady* piece is a "B" on the label with three stars above it, symbolizing top quality. A blue label signifies handblown glass, while red means it is pressed.

Visits: Groups only, booked at least a week in advance. Poděbrady, one of the most accessible of the major glassworks, is only a 45-minute drive from Prague. To get there from Prague, start out from Horní Počernice on the eastern outskirts of the city and take Rte. E67/11 in the direction of Hradec Králové. Poděbrady itself is an interesting old spa town with an equestrian statue of King George of Poděbrady in the center, beautiful parks to wander in, and impressive architecture to gaze at when you've finished admiring the glass. An enjoyable day trip.

Stores: The main store is at the company's administrative headquarters, across from the train station. Tel. (0324) 613 47. Open Mon. 1:30pm-5pm, Tues.-Fri., 9am-12, 12:30pm-5pm. Credit cards, currency exchange office. Next to the factory itself is a smaller shop with mostly machine-made pieces. Open Mon.-Fri. 9am-4:30pm.

In Prague, *Erpet Company* - Staroměstské náměstí 27, Prague 1. Tel. (02) 24 22 97 55. Credit cards, shipping service, currency exchange office. Open daily 10am-8pm.

POLTÁR CRYSTAL

24% PbO

POLTÁR (Slovakia)

Poltár Glassworks Co., Ltd.
(Sklárne Poltár, a.s.)
SK-987 01 Poltár
Tel. (0864) 3151, 2198
Fax   3363, 2228

THIS LARGE, angular complex rises dramatically out of a rural landscape in the heart of Slovakia. *Poltár* was built in 1971 to supplement existing Czech

glass production and provide local jobs. Members of the established glass community had their doubts - there are no skilled glassmakers in that part of Slovakia, they argued, and no glassmaking tradition. But Poltár has been anything but a failure.

The factory serves as an umbrella for three other nearby glassworks, *Zlatno, Katarínska Huta,* and *Málinec.* The *Poltár* plant began by producing both lead crystal and potash glass, but now concentrates solely on lead crystal, both hand and machine-made.

The *Poltár* complex is a joint-stock company that is still state-owned, but privatization is in the wind. Four heart-shaped linden-tree leaves inside a gold goblet make up the *Poltár* logo.

Visits: The *Poltár* factory is located in central Slovakia east of Banská Bystrica. Drive to Lučenec, and follow the signs to Poltár.

Stores: There is a shop at the factory. Open Mon.-Fri. 6:30am-2:30pm.

In Bratislava, *Michel-Glascentrum* - In the pedestrian zone behind the Hotel Forum. Obchodná 44. Tel. (07) 33 49 73. Open Mon.-Fri. 9am-6pm, Sat. till 4pm.

Photographer: Miroslav Vojtěchovský.

ROSICE U BRNA
Crystalex - Rosice Glassworks
CZ-665 15 Rosice u Brna
Tel. (0502) 41 10 47-9
Fax   41 10 89

A FEW YEARS ago you could be sure that virtually every beer mug in every pub in Czechoslovakia came from *Rosice*, a small glassworks not far from the Moravian capital, Brno. With the advent of private enterprise, however, pub-owners are opting for more variety, so *Rosice*'s market domination is in serious jeopardy.

The works is one of four in the Czech Republic that concentrate on pressed glass. (The other three are *Libs* in Libochovice, *Dubí*, and *Heřmanova Huť*.) *Rosice* was founded in 1921, and experienced its greatest boom in the interwar period, when up to 50% of its output was earmarked for export. After World War II, *Rosice* changed hands several times and struggled to keep its head above water. The state took over in 1946 and merged it with another Moravian plant, *Květná*. By the mid-fifties, *Rosice*'s production had started to pick up again, and in the late sixties, it was separated from *Květná* and consolidated with *Sklo Union* (now *Glavunion*), the industrial glass giant in Teplice. By 1971, 80% of its glass was exported, mostly to the Soviet Union. Since then, *Rosice* has found its market niche in the production of inexpensive household glass, such as fruit compote cups that stack, cooking bowls, candy dishes, and ashtrays, all in amber and pastel colors and designed by Jiří Brabec. After 1989, Soviet demand for *Rosice* glass fell sharply, and the enterprise was forced to look elsewhere for markets. In 1990 it joined *Crystalex*.

Its beer mugs, tumblers, sugar-

Photo: *Crystalex.*

bowls, ashtrays, wine bottles, and other household items are made by pressing the hot glass mass into a metal mould. *Rosice* is still the only glassworks in the Czech or Slovak Republics that makes classic beer mugs on an automatic production line, and is virtually the sole source of pressed household glass in solid colors. Its other products include bricks, roof tiles, technical glass, and hotel and restaurant glassware.

Visits: Visitors are welcome, but are asked to phone a week in advance. The town of Rosice is located 20 km west of Brno on the main Brno-Prague highway. Get off at the Kývalka or Ostrovačice exits and follow the signs to Rosice. The factory is near the train station.

Stores: *Rosice* beer mugs can be purchased in Prague's *Kotva* department store and in selected *Crystalex* shops. The rest of its glassware is only sold wholesale, primarily to restaurants.

ŠKRDLOVICE

Beránek Glassworks
(Beránek s.r.o.)
Sklářská Huť, CZ-592 21
Škrdlovice 130
Tel. (0616) 992 31
Fax   991 33

ERÁNEK is the only Czech glassworks focusing solely on contemporary-looking decorative objects. This is designer glass par excellence. Every piece that bears the Beránek label is handmade, most of it hot-shaped without the use of moulds, and almost all of it unconventional. There are glass toothpaste tubes

Photographer: Miroslav Vojtěchovský.

with translucent red and blue stripes, glass fruit so realistic that you want to eat it, surrealistic flowers on long glass stems, ingenious paperweights, lyrical candlesticks. Most of the glass bowls and vases are utilitarian, but you wouldn't want to use them - they're too beautiful.

The *Beránek* works was started in 1940 by Emanuel Beránek, a glassmaker who had returned to his native Moravia from Nový Bor when the Nazis marched into the Sudetenland. With his three brothers, Beránek used whatever materials he could find to make glass. His first attempts were so full of bubbles that he decided to make the look intentional. This pseudo-antique glass found buyers, but he was eventually forced to close the works during the German occupation. After the liberation of Czechoslovakia it was reopened, only to be claimed by the Communists in 1949.

The glassworks was too small and offbeat to fit into the state's industrial plans, so it was consigned to liquidation. *Beránek* had its supporters, though, and they launched a lobbying campaign to save it. The state relented, and the factory, now stripped of the Beránek name, was designated a craft center under the Ministry of Culture. As it was not allowed to make the kind of glass produced by the bigger factories, the logical solution was a new orientation towards art glass. Noted artists such as František Vízner, Miluše Roubíčková, Jaroslav Svoboda,

and Emanuel Beránek's son, Jan, have all designed for the works at Škrdlovice. In 1970, it hosted an international glass symposium devoted to hot-shaped techniques, and other symposia followed.

In 1992, the factory was returned to the Beránek family under the property restitution law. So far it is the only glassworks to have been given back, rather than sold, to its original owners. It is currently managed by Vlastimil Beránek, Emanuel's grandson, who trained under Stanislav Libenský.

The *Beránek* logo is a white ram on a red background, inspired by the company name, which means "little ram."

Visits: Visitors are welcome, but are asked to call in advance. Škrdlovice is north of Žďár nad Sázavou.

Stores: There is a shop at the factory. Open Mon.-Fri. 9am-5pm.

In Prague, *Dialog Art* - Hybernská 1, Prague 1. Tel. (02) 235 64 35. Open Mon.-Fri. 10am-8pm, Sat.-Sun. till 5pm.

Terra Nova - Jindřišská 19, Prague 1. Tel. (02) 26 83 82. Open Mon.-Fri. 10am-6pm, Sat. till 1pm. *Jafa* - Maiselova 15, Prague 1. Tel. (02) 231 00 40. Open daily 9am-7pm.

Melissa - Pařížská 3, Prague 1. Tel. (02) 232 58 06. Open Sun.-Wed. 9am-9pm, Thur.-Sat till 11pm, and Mostecká 24, Prague 1. Tel. (02) 53 16 75. Open Mon.-Wed. 9am-11pm, Thurs.-Sat. 9am- midnight.

SMRŽOVKA

Elegant
CZ-468 51 Smržovka
Tel. (0428) 666 41
Fax   667 10

ELEGANT is the largest producer of glass buttons in the former Czechoslovakia. Some 50% of its output is made up of buttons, and about half of them are exported. Although they are entirely of glass, some of the buttons look as if they could be of metal or even wood, and many have an old-fashioned charm.

Since the 1989 revolution, the designers have been drawing on styles of the 1940s and 1950s for inspiration. All *Elegant* buttons are hand-cut and hand-painted. They are produced by melting the end of a glass rod into a metal mould. (The rods still come from the *Desná* works, as they have since the latter was owned by the Riedel family.) Once the desired shape is obtained, the button is left to cool. It is then cut, polished, and painted.

A number of the button styles double as earrings, but *Elegant* also makes a separate jewelry line of beaded dangling earrings and necklaces. Reflective road signs represent further diversification.

Elegant was originally a group of private producers. It was nationalized after World War II, and made part of the *Skleněná bižuterie* state enterprise in 1953. In 1991,

Elegant broke off and went its own way. Its plant in Hraničná was sold to a private company in the first half of 1993, and its two remaining plants in Smržovka are expected to be privatized by the end of 1993.

The glass rods used in button production. Photographer: Ondřej Kavan.

Visits: Group tours can be arranged by phoning ahead.

Stores: In Smržovka, the company store is on the main square. Open Mon.-Fri. 9am-3pm. Tel. (0428) 666 47.

In Prague, *Knoflíkový ráj* - "Button Paradise." In the shopping passage next to the Estates Theatre (Stavovské divadlo). Open Mon.-Fri. 9:30am-6:30pm, Sat. till 1pm. Tel. (02) 26 38 96.

SMRŽOVKA

Chandelier Glass
(Lustrové sklo)
CZ-468 51 Smržovka

Tel. (0428) 665 41, 665 42,
            665 43, 669 05, 669 44
Fax   667 47
Telex   184456

Photo: *Lustrové sklo.*

LUSTROVÉ SKLO is one of the smaller Czech chandelier producers. What sets it apart is that its sparkling chandelier trimmings contain no lead and are still cut and polished entirely by hand. Unlike its rivals, *Lustrové sklo* complements its lighting fixtures with a special range of unusual glass items: jade glass, elegant flute-cut vases and bowls (with 6% lead content), acid-matted statuettes, figurines made from chandelier trimmings, vases reminiscent of *Moser* in alexandrite (violet), ruby, smoke, citrine, and four other gem colors, and assorted hollow (household) glass. The factory gets its blanks and glass raw materials from the *Ornela* plant in Desná.

Where the artistry comes in is in the cutting, polishing, and decoration. Even its solid brass chandelier frames are handmade and hand-polished. Some 30% of *Lustrové sklo's* production is chandelier trimmings sold as semi-finished products to other important chandelier producing companies, such as *Lustry* at Kamenický Šenov. The jade glass urns and vases and acid-matted statuettes (exposed to hydrofluoric acid to give them a frosted appearance) are based on styles from the 1930s.

Lustrové sklo was privatized as part of a joint venture in October 1993.

The company logo is three crystals on a gold background, representing the opulent cut

glass that goes into its chandeliers.

Visits: Groups are welcome if they phone in advance. There is no glassblowing here, but the hand-cutting of chandelier trimmings can be observed.

Stores: There is no factory store. In Karlovy Vary, *Kvadrant* - Next to the Hotel Dvořák at Nová louka 9. Open Mon.-Sat. 10am-8pm, Sun. 11am-8pm. Tel. (017) 227 59.

SVĚTLÁ NAD SÁZAVOU

Bohemia Glass
(Sklo Bohemia)
Zámecká 550
CZ-582 91 Světlá nad Sázavou)
Tel. (0451) 525 21
Fax   527 91
Telex   196334

S KLO BOHEMIA at Světlá nad Sázavou makes classic hand-blown cut crystal in a wide range of exquisite platters, vases, punch bowls, decanters, stemware, bowls, etc. The vast majority of this glass is exported under the name "Bohemia."

The company has worked for many years with the *Josefodol* glasshouse a few miles away, and continues in that factory's 200-year tradition. Yet it is the youngest of the four largest Czech producers of 24% lead crystal, and boasts the most modern plant and equipment.

Established in 1967, it formed part of the *Bohemia* monolith until 1991, when it split off and became an independent joint-stock company. Cut crystal from Světlá nad Sázavou differs little from that made at *Sklárny Bohemia* in Poděbrady, although more automatic production is done at Světlá

nad Sázavou - on the order of 40,000 pieces a day.

Sklo Bohemia opened a beautiful new shop in 1992 on Na příkopě in downtown Prague, its eighth in the Czech Republic. The best prices, of course, are at the factory.

The company logo is a solid black "B" on a gold background, with a gold star on its upper half.

Visits: Visitors are welcome to come and watch the glass being made Mon.-Fri. 6am-2pm. Please phone ahead. From Prague, take the Brno highway to Humpolec, then follow the signs for "Světlá n. S." It's 20 minutes from the highway. Once in town, drive straight around the castle (now an agricultural secondary school), without crossing the bridge. From a distance you can see the tall smokestack beckoning.

For a lovely view of the countryside, take a short detour on the way back to Prague. Turn left off the main road when you see the sign "Lipence n. S." The road winds through thick forests for 7 km. When you emerge you'll see a stunning castle on the crest of a hill, surrounded by an idyllic, unspoiled cobblestoned village.

124

There are spectacular 365 degree views from the castle.

Stores: There is a shop at the factory. It carries seconds only. Zámecká 550. Tel. (0451) 514 36. Open Mon.-Fri. 8am-2pm. Closed the last two weeks in July and the first week of August.

In Světlá nad Sázavou, *Sklo Bohemia* - Company store.

Naměstí Trčků z Lípy. Tel. (0451) 512 12. Open Mon.-Fri. 9am-4:15pm. Credit cards, currency exchange office.

In Prague, *Sklo Bohemia* - Na příkopě 17, Prague 1. Tel. (02) 222 465. Open Mon.-Fri. 9am-7pm, Sat. 10am-4pm Credit cards, currency exchange office.

TASICE

Jacob Works, Tasice
(Huť Jakub Tasice)
CZ-584 01 Ledeč nad Sázavou
Tel. (0452) 2723
        (0327) 926 25
Fax (02) 72 80 28

THIS SMALL, rustic glassworks provided the setting for the popular 1985 Czech television series *The Sons and Daughters of Jacob the Glassblower*, about the life and times of a glassmaking community in 1899. The works itself, which is nestled in the middle of a village, was founded in 1796. A look at the wooden planking inside gives you an idea of what glassmaking must have been like a century ago.

In the early 19th century, *Tasice* made a name for itself as a supplier of high-quality glass for the decorating workshops in the Nový Bor and Kamenický Šenov region. Its most prosperous period was in the latter part of the century, when its glass was sold throughout Europe. After it was nationalized at the end of World War II, *Tasice* was placed under the

Bohemia conglomerate. In 1957 the government decided to merge it with the *Kavalier Glassworks*, the producer of flame-proof kitchenware.

Under its new owner, Petr Moidl, the *Jacob Works* makes hand-prepared glass panels that are sold to artists. It is also experimenting with blown glass, making brightly colored vases, ashtrays, goblets, and decorated items. A café has been installed in the balcony overlooking the production hall so that visitors can watch the glassmaking process in comfort.

Visits: Unannounced visitors are welcome Mon.-Fri. 8am-2pm, but a phone call in advance would be appreciated if you're planning to have lunch in the café. The *Jacob Works* is a 30 km drive north of the Prague-Brno highway, not far from *Sklo Bohemia* at Světlá nad Sázavou. Take the Loket or Koberovice exits and drive north to Ledeč nad Sázavou. Follow the signs to Jedlá-Tasice, about 10 km to the north.

Stores: There is a shop at the factory. Open Mon.-Fri. 8am-2pm.

Photographer:
Miroslav
Vojtěchovský.

VALAŠSKÉ MEZIŘÍČÍ

Illuminating Glass
(Osvětlovací sklo, a.s.)
CZ-757 25 Valašské Meziříčí
Tel. (0651) 211 89
Fax   218 34
Telex   52218, 52869

OSVĚTLOVACÍ SKLO is the largest Czech manufacturer of contemporary glass lighting fixtures. It also makes glass parts for automotive headlights and reflectors, and for many years was a major producer of glass components for television screens. Indeed, it was one of the first factories in Europe to produce them. For four decades it exported about 30% of its output to other countries within the Soviet bloc. With the loss of those markets, *Osvětlovací sklo* has found itself in a state of limbo, forced to rethink its marketing strategy.

The factory was founded in 1854 in Valašské Meziříčí (formerly called Krásno nad Bečvou) as one of several glassworks belonging to the *Reich* company. At first it

produced cut and painted glass, but the development of gas lighting created a worldwide demand for glass lamps which *Reich* decided to fill. By the end of the century the firm was known internationally and had sales outlets in Prague and seven other European cities. With the advent of electricity, the company adapted its fixtures and sales continued to soar. In 1934, however, *Reich* went bankrupt, and the factory was divided.

After its nationalization in the postwar period, the factory was amalgamated with eight other local glassworks. In the early 1950s, it began producing pharmaceutical and automotive glass in addition to its line of lamps. After the Velvet Revolution in 1989, the five plants that made up *Osvětlovací sklo* went their own way. Apart from the main factory in Valašské Meziříčí, they included Janštejn, Rapotín, Vsetín, and Košťany. In 1992 the government decided to privatize

Osvětlovací sklo. The lamp and automotive branch and the television screen division in the Valašské Meziříčí complex were split up. A public tender was opened, and the former was acquired in January 1993 by the Czech company Lares, Ltd. *Osvětlovací sklo - Lares, Ltd.,* as the firm is now called, has no plans to change the product lines. The television screen plant, unable to compete with foreign producers, was closed in 1993.

Visits: Visitors are asked to phone at least one week in advance. The factory is on the northeast side of town, under the smokestacks.

Stores: There is a shop next to the factory, *Mio Prodejna Svítidel* - Zašovská 764, Valašské Meziříčí. Tel. (0651) 226 42. Open Mon.-Sat. 8am-6pm, Sat. till 12pm.

In Olomouc, *Mio* - Ulice 8 Května 8. Tel. (068) 52 23 608. Open Mon.-Fri. 8am-6pm, Sat. till 12pm.

Osvětlovací sklo lamps are sold in most Prague lighting shops. *Luna* - Na příkopě 16, Prague 1. Open Mon.-Fri. 9am-7pm, Sat. till 4pm. Tel.: (02) 22 18 39. Credit cards.

Svítidla - Next to *Kotva.* Královdvorská 12, Prague 1 . Tel. (02) 24 22 44 23. Open Mon.-Fri. 10am-5pm.

Superlux - Hybernská 32, Prague 1. Tel. (02) 24 21 35 17. Open Mon.-Fri. 8:30am-6pm, Sat. 9am-12pm.

Bílá Labuť - Na poříčí 23, Prague 1. Tel. (02) 24 81 13 64. Open Mon.-Fri. 8am-7pm, Sat. till 4pm.

VČELNIČKA

Antonín Rückl and Sons, Ltd.
(Antonín Rückl a synové s.r.o.)
CZ-394 70 Včelnička
Tel. (0364) 25 81-4
Fax   24 44

THIS GLASSWORKS is the third of those bought back by the Rückl family in 1992. Unlike *Nižbor*, which produces 24% lead crystal, and *Skalice u České Lípy*, which makes eyeglass lenses, this works specializes in luxury colored glass. Its lines include red stemware with painted flowers, colored paneled goblets with fine gilt *lištovačka* decoration, and more modern designs. The glass is blown at *Včelnička* and trucked to a yellow stucco manor in the village of Kamenice nad Lipou 3 km to the north for painting and decorating.

Antonín Rückl leased the plant in 1875 and began producing plain glass. It was shipped by rail to the decorating workshops in Haida (Nový Bor) and Steinschönau (Kamenický Šenov). Three years later he established a glass-cutting workshop at the factory, expanding its workforce to 100 cutters by 1887. *Rückl* colored glass was exported throughout Europe, and the Rückls purchased the factory on the eve of World War I.

Business thrived between the wars, but after World War II, the glasshouse was nationalized and later merged with *Česky křišťál* in Chlum u Třeboně. Ultimately it was brought under the aegis of the *Crystalex* corporation.

Včelnička could not be returned to the Rückls under the property restitution law because the company had been nationalized before the stipulated cutoff date of 1948. Consequently, in 1992 the Rückl

Photo: *Antonín Rückl and Sons Ltd.*

family purchased it from the state. Jan Rückl, a manager at *Crystalex* for 14 years, is now director of the works. A local glassmaker, Miroslav Lenc, found a dusty old *Rückl* sample book dating from 1915 in an attic, and the factory has drawn on the delicately colored sketches for ideas in developing its newest line of glassware. It is also experimenting with contemporary designs.

VIZOVICE

Glass Atelier Morava
Trikamo, a.s. Zlín
P.O. Box 78
CZ-763 12 Vizovice
Tel. (067) 95 24 84
         95 28 59
Fax   95 28 59

GLASS *Atelier Morava* was the first private glassworks established in Czechoslovakia after the 1989 revolution.

Visits: Visitors are welcome, but are asked to phone in advance.

Stores: In Kamenice nad Lipou, *Rückl a synové* - Náměstí české armády 53. Tel. (0364) 28 05. Open Mon.-Fri. 8am-11:30am, 2pm-4pm, Sat. till 11am.

In Prague, *Rückl & Sons* - Dlouhá třída 19, Prague 1. Tel. (02) 232 36 48. Open Mon.-Fri. 10am-7pm, Sat. till 2pm. Credit cards.

The new company Trikamo, a.s. built the factory from scratch in the town of Vizovice outside the Moravian shoe-manufacturing town of Zlín.

Trikamo was determined to operate a modern, energy-efficient, environmentally-friendly plant producing high-quality stemware designed to satisfy Western tastes. They brought in state-of-the-art equipment from Germany and lead-free raw materials from the Netherlands. Then they recruited the best local talent they could find. They lured award-winning glass designer Jiří Vosmík away from the *Vrbno* works and hired skilled glassblowers from nearby plants.

Within its very first year, *Glass Atelier Morava* was already a resounding success. Its glassware is sophisticated, with unusually long, slender stems and colorful accents. The word has spread to upscale European buyers, particularly in Germany, Italy, and Greece, and North and South American buyers are also starting to catch on. Many companies in the Czech Republic produce contemporary stemware, but that of *Glass Atelier Morava* is in a class of its own.

Visits: Visitors are welcome to stop at the factory and watch the glass being blown, but are asked to phone in advance.

Stores: *Glass Atelier Morava* items can be bought directly from the factory Mon.-Fri. 7am-4pm.

The following shops in Prague carry selected lines: *Philadelphia-*Vodičkova 30, Prague 1. Tel. (02) 235 84 42. Open Mon.-Sat. 9am-7pm.
Dialog Art – Hybernská 1, Prague 1. Tel. (02) 235 64 35. Open Mon.-Fri. 10am-8pm, Sat.-Sun. till

Photo: *Glass Atelier Morava.*

5pm. *Cristallino* - Celetná 12, Prague 1. Tel. (02) 22 83 66. Open daily 9am-8pm. You can see *Glass Atelier Morava's* full product range in its showroom at Žitná 8, Prague 2, but no glass can be purchased there. Tel. (02) 29 98 67, 29 92 19.

VRBNO POD PRADĚDEM

Crystalex - Vrbno Works
CZ-793 26 Vrbno pod Pradĕdem
Tel. (0646) 522 13-15
Fax   527 15

V RBNO is a small glassworks located up north in the foothills of Moravia's Jeseníky Mountains. Perhaps it's by virtue of its sheer remoteness that it has developed such an individual style. *Vrbno* stemware always seems a little freer, more artistic than the competition's. Characteristic are the curlicued stems, the offbeat shapes, and unusual color combinations.

    The glassworks was founded in 1862 by Rudolf Richter and initially produced hand-pressed glass. At the end of the 19th century it expanded into glassblowing, and a painting and glass-cutting workshop was opened. The works turned out Art Nouveau styles to satisfy American, British, and Italian customers, but later shifted full tilt towards the Middle East and began producing painted glass with Islamic motifs. One of the biggest successes was a line of "Persian tumblers." After World War I, sales plunged. By selling shares to the public, *Richter & Co.* managed to coast through the Depression years, continually adapting to satisfy market demands.

    The works was nationalized in 1945, and a 20-year odyssey of bureaucratic reorganization began. First *Vrbno* was placed under the *Bohemian-Moravian*

Glassworks collective, then under the *Rapotín Glassworks*. In 1958 it was regrouped with *Kvĕtná* and *Karolinka*, and three years later it was put under the *Moravian Glassworks National Corporation*. It ended up as part of *Crystalex*. Its facilities were modernized in the 1960s to produce painted, cut, and etched drinking sets. In the

Photographer: Lumír Rott.

130

1970s, Jiří Vosmík started designing offbeat models, and *Vrbno* took on a new identity. Although Vosmík left in 1992 to work for *Glass Atelier Morava*, *Vrbno* continues to come out with appealing models thanks to designer Božena Glončáková.

The company logo is a round black flower poised over the top of a black goblet.

Visits: Visitors are welcome Monday through Friday, 7am-12pm.

Advance booking required. From Prague, *Vrbno* is a six-hour drive along country roads, but the scenery is lovely and there are a number of country hotels en route.

Stores: There is a shop at the factory. Open Mon.-Fri. 8am-6pm. *Vrbno* glass is also sold in selected Crystalex stores.

Holders of GWC cards get a 5% discount on glass in the factory store.

Photographer: Gabriel Urbánek.

VSETÍN

Bohemia Art Glass, s. r. o.
Bobrky 426
P. O. Box 16
CZ-755 01 Vsetín
Tel. (0657) 7764, 7432, 81083
Fax   2048

THIS brand-new glassworks is one of the most talked-about in the Czech Republic. Its hot-shaped, moulded household glass is delightfully inventive: wildly colorful goblets on tall, unconventional stems, tumblers with paperweights as bases, and artistic vases are just a preview of what lies in store. This is probably the closest that any Czech producer currently comes to the colorful styles produced in Murano, Italy.

Bohemia Art Glass (*BAG* for short) is owned by seven glass specialists who also run *Glass Service*, which provides technical services in industrial glass and expertise in the construction of glass furnaces. In January 1993, the group recruited the area's best glassblowers and started manufacturing glassware, even while its premises were still under construction. A number of artists, including Jiří Šuhájek, are designing for *BAG*, which has already attracted the interest of buyers in Sweden and the United States.

Visits: This works is highly accessible. Visitors are welcome

to arrive unannounced anytime from Mon.-Fri. 6am-2pm and watch the glassblowing from a balcony overlooking the main hall. Driving south from Valašské Meziříčí on Rte. 57, you'll find the works on the left-hand side of the road just a few kilometers outside Vsetín, opposite a service station. Closed mid-July to mid-August.

While you're in the area, drive over to the open-air folk museum in Rožnov pod Radhoštěm, which provides an idea of life as it used to be in the rural villages of the hilly region known as Moravian Wallachia.

Stores: There is a shop at the factory.

In Prague, *Melissa* - Pařížská 3, Prague 1. Tel. (02) 23 26 06. Open daily 9am-9pm. *Melissa* - Mostecká 24, Prague 1. Tel. (02) 53 16 75. Open Mon.-Wed. 9am-11pm, Thurs.-Sat. till midnight.

ZÁSADA

*Ornela, a.s. -
division Czech Beads*
(Ornela, a.s. -
divize České perličky)
CZ-468 25 Zásada
Tel. (0428) 932 41
Fax   936 31

THIS FACTORY makes the miniature beads known as "rocaille," or "seed beads," that are so commonly found in Native American art. Less well known is the fact that many of the beads these Indian tribes were sewing into their leather moccasins and clothing in the nineteenth century actually came from Bohemia and were shipped to North America by European traders.

České perličky is the world's largest single producer of seed beads; it currently has a 20% share of the world market. Its biggest competitors are Taiwan, China, and Japan, but there is no single factory in those countries producing the quantity or assortment that this one does. *České perličky* beads range in size from the minuscule (1 mm) to Tic Tac size (about 4 mm). They come matte, transparent, or with metallic or alabaster coatings. There are gold- and silver-lined beads and clear beads with colored centers. The factory sells them by the kilo, but also strings them into its own creative jewelry. *České perličky* necklaces come in every hue of the color scale - braided, woven,

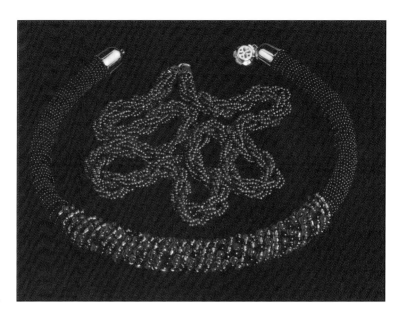

Photographer:
Gabriel Urbánek.

or hanging loose in oodles of delicate strands.

In 1993, *České perličky* formed a private joint-stock company together with its glass supplier, *Desenské sklárny*. The company now goes under the name *Ornela*.

Visits: No tours of the production hall are possible.

Stores: There is a shop at the factory, where prices are lower and the selection is far wider than in retail stores. Open Mon.-Fri. 8am-4pm. Tel. (0428) 932 41.

ŽELEZNÝ BROD

Estrela, a.s.
CZ-468 22 Železný Brod - Tepeře
Tel. (0428) 727 41-45
Fax   724 26

ESTRELA is one of only two producers of imitation pearls in the Czech Republic (the other is the *Železný Brod Glass* factory). Within three years, this relatively small privatized company has opened up branch offices in the West and watched its turnover double, making it one of the most successful costume jewelry companies to emerge from the former Czechoslovakia. It has set up its own bank, installed a sophisticated computer system, erected new facilities, and acquired enough resources to make itself almost self-sufficient in glass raw materials.

Before the 1989 revolution, the *Estrela* plant was one of eight working under *Železnobrodské sklo*. In July 1990, 11 of its employees formed a company and bought the plant from the state. To learn about Western sales and management techniques, the owners went on internships with businesses in Western Europe and the United States. Then they returned to Tepeře and applied their newly acquired knowledge. The rest is history.

Curiously, solid glass imitation pearls as produced today weren't invented until the 1920s. In the 16th century, craftsmen devised a way of blowing a small glass bubble and filling it with hot wax. The white wax shining through its glass exterior looked something like a pearl. But these first imitation pearls were fragile. Later, glassblowers pressed alabaster glass into bead moulds, yielding a stronger product with a more pearl-like appearance. Today's beads are solid glass of a much tougher constitution, although they are still called "waxed beads" by those in the trade. The secret lies in concocting a chemical coating that gleams like mother-of-pearl.

Estrela was founded in 1892 by Josef Hásek, one of many entrepreneurs in the Jablonec region engaged in costume jewelry production. Glass jewelry was always a lucrative field because it was hugely popular as an inexpensive substitute for coveted gemstones. The name was taken from a color chart: "estrela" was a greenish-turquoise bead that is still produced at the factory today.

Estrela makes up to 300 different shapes, sizes, and colors of imitation pearls. The enduring color favorites are classic white and cream. It also produces opaque and marbled beads. Jewelry styles range from the simple strand of pearls to designer creations embellished with sparkling stones, gold, and silver.

Visits: No tours of the production hall are possible.

Stores: There is a shop at the factory. Open Mon.-Fri. 8am-5pm. From Železný Brod, drive towards Jablonec nad Nisou and turn left at the sign for Tepeře.

In Prague, *Estrela* pieces are available in most costume jewelry shops, such as *Royal* at Na příkopě 12, Prague 1. Tel. (02) 24 21 05 52. Open Mon.-Sat. 9am-7pm, Sun. 10am-7pm.

ŽELEZNÝ BROD

Liglass
CZ-468 22 Železný Brod
Tel. (0428) 772 41
Fax   772 72

LIGLASS, which split off from the Železný Brod glassworks in 1990 to form its own joint--stock company, is one of the world's largest producers of partly-cut glass jewelry stones and beads. *Liglass* beads are distinctive for their size: big, often clear or partly clear, and in unusual colors and shapes.

While still part of the *Železnobrodské sklo* complex, *Liglass* concentrated on technical glass, glass jewelry, beads, and jewelry-related semifinished products. Since its independence, it has branched out into other areas, including chandeliers, lamps, plastic toys, games, and fashion accessories.

Up until the 1950s, the *Liglass* premises were a textile factory. The facilities were remodeled, and jewelry-making became the main activity. After 1958, the factory supervised a local network of home-

Photo: *Liglass.*

based bead and jewelry producers that rivaled that other great center of Bohemian costume jewelry, Jablonec nad Nisou. It is now the country's only producer of partially-cut glass stones, and one of only a few that make doublets, which are two crystals cemented together with a layer of colored glass between them. *Liglass* especially stands out for its lamp beads, which come in over 10,000 different shapes and colors. These beads are made by dipping the tip of a long iron rod into the molten glass, and winding the viscous glass around the rod to form a bead. The bead is then knocked off and allowed to cool.

Visits: No factory visits are possible.

Stores: Unfortunately for bead-lovers, individual *Liglass* beads are not available in bulk on the domestic market, but their costume jewelry is sold in several shops.

In Prague, *Lustry, Sklo, Nábytek* - Facing the Vltava at Masarykovo nábřeží 6, Prague 2.
Open Mon.-Fri. 9:30am-6pm, Sat. 8:30am-4pm, Sun. 1:30pm-5pm.
Royal - Na příkopě 12, Prague 1. Tel. (02) 24 21 05 52.
Open Mon.-Sat. 9am-7pm, Sun. 10am-7pm. *Jafa* - Maiselova 15, Prague 1.
Tel. (02) 231 00 40.
Open daily 9am-7pm. *Luna* - *Liglass* chandeliers. Na příkopě 16, Prague 1.
Open Mon.-Fri. 9am-7pm, Sat. till 4pm.
Tel. (02) 22 18 39.

ŽELEZNÝ BROD
Železný Brod Glass
(Železnobrodské sklo)
Průmyslová 702, CZ-468 22
Železný Brod
Tel. (0428) 76 62 57
Fax 76 65 01
Telex 186237

THE CENTER of glassmaking in Železný Brod is the Železnobrodské sklo glassworks, producing several exclusive styles of hot-shaped glass, as well as a broad range of costume jewelry, chandeliers, and cut and engraved glass. This is also where the country's most famous glass artists - Stanislav Libenský and Jaroslava Brychtová - have their sculptures made.

But the factory's real claim to fame is something else entirely: glass figurines. No other Czech glassworks produces them. The smaller ones, which are about 7 cm (3 in.) high, are made by heating small rods of colored glass over a flame. The larger ones, which can be up to 20 cm (8 in.) in height, are shaped directly at the furnace. The detail in these glass creations is nothing short of amazing. Among the most popular is a set of glass physicians, including a general practitioner preparing a syringe and an obstetrician holding a newborn baby. There are also musicians, pirates, animals of all species, and Cinderella-style glass slippers.

Jaroslava Brychtová's father, Jaroslav Brychta, pioneered figurine production at the *Železný Brod* works. Some of his original pieces are in the Ethnographic Museum in the town square.

Železnobrodské sklo was established in 1948, when the state nationalized and consolidated a group of small-scale glass producers in the area. Nine factories were ultimately merged into one, five of them dealing in costume jewelry. In 1955, a small furnace was built in the nearby secondary school of glassmaking for use by the school and for production purposes. In 1965, the spacious factory used today went into operation, employing about 1,500. Since 1991, its subsidiaries have split off into independent companies. They include *Estrela*, *Astir*, *Liglass*, *Skleněná bižuterie*, *Slovbijoux*, *Elegant*, and *BTV*, a producer of plastic jewelry. The main works, which continues to produce figurines, flame-polished beads, the raw materials for imitation pearls, chandeliers, cut glass, engraved glass, contemporary hot-shaped vases and animal figures, became a joint stock company in 1994.

Visits: No tours of the production hall are possible.

Stores: In Železný Brod, *Železnobrodské sklo* - The company store, on the main square at náměstí Května 3. Tel. (0428) 728 89. Open Mon.-Fri. 8am-6pm, Sat. till 12pm.

In Prague, *Krystal* - On the corner of Vodičkova ulice at Václavské náměstí 30, Prague 1. Tel. (02) 26 33 84. Open Mon.-Fri. 9am-7pm, Sat. till 4pm. Credit cards.

Mirea-Shop - Na příkopě 25, Prague 1. Tel. (02) 24 22 81 62. Open daily 9am-8pm. Credit cards, shipping service.

Photographers: Zdenka Kalabisová and Antonín Krčmář.

ŽELIEZOVCE (Slovakia)

Slovbijoux, s.p.
Námestie Februárového
víťazstva 17
SK-937 01 Želiezovce,
Tel. (0811) 2479
Fax   2529
Telex   76322

SLOVBIJOUX is Slovakia's only producer of glass costume jewelry, including handmade beads and imitation pearls. Jewelry production began here in 1963, but for almost 30 years this manufacturer produced semifinished products for a large Czech costume jewelry enterprise and had no identity of its own.

The idea of producing glass jewelry in Slovakia originated in Prague. The state concluded that the giant *Jablonecká bižuterie* corporation could use an alternative source of beads and semifinished products to use in the production of its jewelry, then traded exclusively through the state jewelry exporting company, *Jablonex.* Želiezovce, a town of about 7,500 inhabitants in an agricultural region in southeastern Slovakia, was chosen as the site.

The workforce at first strung necklaces by hand. Later mechanical stringing machines were introduced and the beadmakers worked at home. In 1966, the factory installed machines to grind and press beads. New stringing workshops were built, and older ones were expanded. Many of these colorful Slovak-made beads were shipped to the *České perličky* plant in Zásada, northern Bohemia, where they were woven into necklaces together with Zásada's tiny "seed beads." Another building was added to the Želiezovce complex in 1976, and imitation pearls went into production. In 1977, the factory was placed under the costume jewelry branch of the *Železnobrodské sklo.* But this conglomerate split up in 1991, and the Želiezovce plant went its own way. The Slovak government renamed the factory *Slovbijoux.*

The works, with 285 employees, remains state-owned for the time being.

It continues to produce beads, jewelry, and buttons. The plant is located a few kilometers from the Hungarian border, due north of Budapest.

Visits: No factory tours are possible.

Stores: The beads and jewelry can be bought at the factory Mon.-Fri. 7am-4pm.

ZLATNO (Slovakia)

Poltár Glassworks Co., Ltd. - Zlatno
(Sklárne Poltár, a.s.
Závod Zlatno u Lučence)
SK-951 91 Zlatno
Tel. (0864) 3151
Fax   3363

OF ALL the glassworks still producing stemware in Slovakia, this is the oldest. Founded in 1836 by Johann Georg Zahn, who also operated glassworks in Bohemia, the factory made luxury household glass and stemware from the very beginning. It also manufactured some of the first mirrors in the region. *Zahn* glass was decorated, hot-shaped, and cut on the wheel.

In 1847, a Polish chemist employed at the factory, Leopold Valentin Pantoczek, won international prizes for discovering new glass decorating techniques. Chief

SLOVAKIA
GLASS

1 8 3 6

Photographer: Miroslav Vojtěchovský.

among them were the techniques of pressing glass between two thin plates into which a relief had been carved, giving it a silvery sheen using a hyaloplastic process, and iridizing glass by applying thin metallic coatings to its surface. This last technique was widely used worldwide in Art Nouveau designs.

After World War II, *Zlatno* was consolidated with other Slovak works under the *Tatrasklo* corporation, and became part of the *Poltár Glassworks* in the early 1970s. Under privatization plans, this plant is to remain within *Poltár* as a joint-stock company, but gain increased independence.

The works currently produces stemware in spare, modern designs and hot-shaped motifs, often in pastel colors. One of its most successful products is the amber-stemmed "Gold Suzanna" set.

Visits: Visitors are welcome Mon.-Fri. 5:30am-1:30pm, if they phone in advance. *Zlatno* is located near Lučenec, southern Slovakia, not far from the Hungarian border.

Stores: There is a shop at the factory. Open Mon.-Fri. 6:30am-1:30pm.

In Bratislava, *Michel Glas Centrum* - Obchodná 44.
Tel. (07) 33 49 73.
Open Mon.-Fri. 9am-6pm, Sat. till 4pm.

INDUSTRIAL GLASS PRODUCERS

Avirunion, a.s.
Sklářská 450, CZ-416 74 Teplice,
Czech Republic.
Tel. (0417) 34 11, Fax 34 22 70.
Pharmaceutical glass, bottles, jars.

Bratislava-Dúbravka
Agátová 22, SK-844 03 Bratislava,
Slovakia.
Tel. (07) 690 01, Fax 76 99 42.
Lead glass tubes, eutalic balls
used to produce glass fibers, and
sound insulation materials.

Clara
SK-985 06 Utekáč, Slovakia.
Tel. (0864) 936 21, Fax 936 13.
Thermos bottles and glass linings
for them, and lamp bulbs.

Glavunion, a.s.
Sklářská 450, CZ-416 74 Teplice,
Czech Republic.
Tel. (0417) 34 11, Fax 277 77.
Float and sheet glass, safety glass,
wire-glass, automotive, architec-
tural and bulletproof glass.

Klára Huť, s.p.
CZ-471 16 Polevsko, Czech
Republic.
Tel. (0424) 20 00, Fax 2612.
Colored sheet glass.

Moravia, a.s.
CZ-696 03 Dubňany, Czech
Republic.
Tel. (0628) 964 96, Fax 962 90.
Large container glass, demijohns.

Moravia, a.s.
CZ-679 39 Úsobrno, Czech
Republic. Tel. (0501) 957 25,
Fax 957 37. Containers and
technical glass.

A. Rückl a synové, a.s.
CZ-471 17 Skalice u České Lípy,
Czech Republic.
Tel. (0424) 318 61, Fax 318 71.
Optical glass, eyeglass lenses.

Severosklo, a.s.
Tkalcovská 182, CZ-473 18 Nový
Bor, Czech Republic.
Tel. (0424) 2545, Fax 2876.
Optical glass, welding and protec-
tive glass.

Sklárny Kavalier, a.s.
Sklářská 359, CZ-285 96 Sázava,
Czech Republic.
Tel. (0328) 913 51, Fax 913 50.
Laboratory and technical glass,
flame-proof kitchenware.

Skloobal Nemšová
SK-914 41 Nemšová, Slovak
Republic.
Tel. (0831) 984 31, Fax 982 16.
Glass jars for foods and phar-
maceutical products.

Skloplast
Strojárenská 1, SK-917 99 Trnava,
Slovakia.
Tel. (0805) 237 91, Fax 244 98.
Glass fibers.

Union-Lesní brána, a.s.
Novosedlická 125, CZ-417 03
Dubí u Teplic,
Czech Republic. Tel. (0417) 3151,
Fax 402 27. Heat-insulating
fiberglass.

Vertex, a.s.
Robkova 51, CZ-570 21 Litomyšl,
Czech Republic.
Tel. (0464) 3311, Fax 3669. Glass
fibers.

Vetropack, Moravia Glass, a.s.
Havlíčkova 180, CZ-697 29
Kyjov, Czech Republic.
Tel. (0629) 2111, Fax 4601. Jars.

Vitrablok, a.s.
Bílinská 42, CZ-419 14 Duchov,
Czech Republic.

Tel. (0417) 93 56 82,
Fax 93 58 07. Glass blocks.

Vsetínské sklárny
Ohrada, CZ-756 01 Vsetín, Czech
Republic. Tel. (0657) 4351, Fax
7542. Glass oil lamps, Dewar
flasks, technical glass.

PRODUCERS OF GLASS CHRISTMAS
TREE DECORATIONS

Astir
Na hutích 26, CZ-466 21 Jablonec
nad Nisou, Czech Republic.
Tel. (0428) 225 69.

Bižuterie, a.s
U přehrady,
CZ-466 23 Jablonec nad Nisou,
Czech Republic.
Tel. (0428) 417 11,
Fax 41 77 01,
Telex 186414.

**Družstvo Vánoční ozdoby
(Christmas Tree Decoration
Cooperative)**
Benešovo nábřeží 2286,
CZ-544 02 Dvůr Králové nad

Labem, Czech Republic.
Tel. (0437) 2126.

Noel
Souběžná 3, CZ-466 01 Jablonec
nad Nisou, Czech Republic.
Tel. (0428) 297 34.

Okrasa Čadca
Matičné námestie 1, SK-02201
Čadca, Slovakia.
Tel. (0824) 230 29
or 230 27.

Opava Slezská tvorba
Sadová 4, CZ-74601 Opava,
Czech Republic.
Tel. (0653) 21 52 50.

PART SIX • RESOURCES

MUSEUMS

SOME of the most valuable glass treasures in the world are found in the provincial museums of the Czech Republic and Slovakia. Although they are only a few hours' drive from Prague, most of these collections are still off the beaten tourist track and you can enjoy them in peace and quiet. A perfect day trip can be had by combining a museum visit with a tour of a nearby glassworks, and, of course, stopping in at the factory store.

The Neo-Renaissance stairwell Prague's *Museum of Decorative Arts* Photo: Museum Photographer: Gabriel Urbáne

Museum of Decorative Arts

(Uměleckoprůmyslové muzeum)
17 listopadu 2
CZ-110 01 Prague 1
Tel. (02) 24 81 12 41,

Open Tues.-Sun. 10am-6pm

The 17th-century engraved crystal on display is a vivid reminder that for the better part of 100 years Bohemian glass was the most highly prized in the world. Besides the stunning examples of Baroque artistry, this collection of 20,000 pieces - the largest exhibit of glass in the Czech Republic - includes enamel-painted Renaissance beakers and Venetian and Spanish glass from the 16th-18th centuries. It all serves to give you a sense of perspective when you make your own purchases.

The museum, located across the street from the Rudolfinum concert hall, also contains antique furniture, porcelain, and silver.

There is a library one flight up. Open to the public Mon. 12pm-6pm, Tues.-Fri. 10am-6pm (closed July-Aug.). The café on the ground floor offers a welcome respite from the dazzling splendor upstairs.

The *Museum of Decorative Arts.* Photographer: Diane Foulds.

Moravian Gallery
(Moravská Galerie)
Husova 14
CZ-662 26 Brno
Tel. (05) 261 51, 237 26
Open Tues.-Sun. 10am-6pm

Housing the second largest glass collection in the Czech Republic after Prague's Museum of Decorative Arts, the Moravian Gallery was also the second museum of applied arts to be founded in the former Austro-Hungarian Empire, after the Österreichisches Museum für Angewandte Kunst in Vienna.

In addition to a beautiful collection of 19th-century goblets from *Harrachov* and other glassworks in northern Bohemia, there is a room devoted to modern glass sculpture by

such stars as Pavel Hlava, František Vízner, and the Stanislav Libenský & Jaroslava Brychtová team.

Museum of Northern Bohemia
(Severočeské muzeum)
Masarykova 11
CZ-460 01 Liberec
Tel. (048) 237 66
Open Tues. 12pm-5pm, Wed.- Sun. 9am-5pm

As you might expect from a city whose streets are lined with the mansions of prewar textile barons, the local museum boasts an impressive collection of richly decorated glass. The museum, founded in 1873 when Liberec, or Reichenberg, was a predominantly German-speaking textile center,

The *Museum of Northern Bohemia*, Liberec. Photo: Museum.

The *Nový Bor Glass Museum.* Photo: Museum. Photographer: Lubomír Hána.

also has jewelry, lace, tapestries, porcelain, furniture, and antique clocks.

There is a gift shop in the museum.

While in the Liberec area, chandelier-lovers might wish to take a short drive out of town to see the massive chandelier in the Church of the Pilgrimage in Hejnice. It dates from 1853 and was manufactured by *Josef Helzel & Co.* of Kamenický Šenov, one of the leading chandelier producers of the day.

Nový Bor Glass Museum
(Sklářské muzeum)
Náměstí Míru 105
CZ-Nový Bor 473 01
Tel. (0424) 321 96
Open Tues.-Sun. 9am-12pm, 1pm-
4pm

The museum was established in 1893 by the leading glassmakers in the region as a showcase for their best work. The collection spans six centuries and innumerable changes in fashion. Today it is housed in a mansion that belonged to a glass trading company, *Hiecke Rautenstrauch Zincke & Co.*, from 1890 to the beginning of World War II. Most of the other buildings on the square, and many on Masarykova ulice, the main street of the town, were also either trading firms or decorating workshops. In 1928, there were over 300 glassworks or decorating workshops in Nový Bor; only a handful still exist. A few of these private companies burned down mysteriously after the state took possession of them in the postwar period.

Replicas of historical models are sold in the museum shop.

Lemberk Castle

(Státní zámek Lemberk)
CZ-471 25 Jablonné v Podještědí
Tel. (0424) 953 05
Open April-Oct., Sat.-Sun. 9am-
4pm, May-Sept., Tues.-Sun. 5pm

This Baroque chateau is only a 15-minute drive from Nový Bor, and well worth a detour to view some of the most interesting avant-garde glass sculptures produced at the international Glass Symposia sponsored by *Crystalex* in 1982, 1985, 1988, and 1991. World-famous glass artists such as Stanislav Libenský & Jaroslava Brychtová, Dale Chihuly, Finn Lynggaard, and Harvey Littleton are represented by their work. The exhibit, on the third floor, is only open during the summer months.

Lemberk Castle, which also has a permanent exhibition on local history, is on the main road (Rte. 13/E442) between Nový Bor and Liberec, just outside Jablonné v Podještědí and visible atop a hill.

Kamenický Šenov Glass Museum

(Sklářské muzeum)
CZ-471 14 Kamenický Šenov
Tel. (0424) 922 06
Open Tues.-Sun. 8:30am-4pm

Exhibited in the former decorating workshops of the famed *J.& L. Lobmeyr Co.*, where some of the best engravers in the world worked in the 19th and early 20th centuries, are 1,000 painted and engraved pieces produced by the firm. *Lobmeyr*, a supplier to the court of Austrian Emperor Franz Josef I, catered to crowned heads and high society throughout Europe. (The company still exists in Austria, with a shop and museum on Vienna's Kärtnerstrasse.)

The museum, in the center of town opposite the church, also houses 2,000 examples of Baroque glassware and a collection of contemporary *Chřibská* glass.

There are two gift shops on the premises.

Museum of Glass and Costume Jewelry

(Muzeum skla a bižuterie)
Jiráskova ulice 4
CZ-466 01 Jablonec nad Nisou
Tel. (0428) 225 22
Open Tues.-Sun. 9am-4pm

While an interesting collection of 19th- and 20th-century glass is also on hand, the main draw is the costume jewelry, for which Jablonec (formerly Gablonz) has been world-famous since the second half of the last century. Many ornate examples of 19th-century glass necklaces, brooches, buttons, and hatpins can be seen here.

The museum is off a side street on the lower of the two squares below the ochre town hall clock-tower.

Museum of Glassmaking in the Jizera Mountains

(Památník sklářství v Jizerských horách)
CZ-460 05 Kristiánov
Open June- Sept., Sat.-Sun. 8am-
5pm

This cozy log cabin - a former pub - is the only surviving trace of the glassmaking settlement of Kristiánov (in German, Christian-thal). In 1964, the Jablonec Museum of Glass and Jewelry opened an exhibition here on the history of glassmaking in the Jizera (Iser) Mountains. A miniature model shows how the village used to look, and regional glassworks, then built in wood, are documented in old pictures.

The Riedel family built a works in Christianthal in 1776, which was destroyed in a forest fire in 1887. But it wasn't until 1938, when another fire gutted the Riedel mansion (then in use as a children's convalescent home), that the village was abandoned.

Drive north from Josefův Důl and look for the sign.

Šumava Museum

(Muzeum Šumavy)
Hlavní náměstí
CZ-341 92 Kašperské Hory
Tel. (0187) 92 25 05
Open May-Oct., Tues.-Sun. 9am-5pm, Nov.-April, Sat. 10am-2pm, or by appointment

Lovers of *Jugendstil*, or Art Nouveau, will revel in the fine examples of the style exhibited in this quaint museum of glass and folk art from the still unspoiled Šumava region (in German, Böhmerwald, or Bohemian Forest). The *Johann Loetz Witwe* glassworks of Klášterský Mlýn (Klostermühle) reached the height of its fame at the turn of the century with iridescent vases rivaling those of Tiffany and Gallé. Viennese artists who designed for the company included Josef Hoffmann and Koloman Moser. It was the first glassworks in Bohemia to produce Art Deco glass. *Loetz* was hurt by the Great Depression, but it shut down for good in 1947, not long after its postwar nationalization. The factory burned down shortly thereafter.

The superb assortment of regionally made multi-colored snuff bottles is another reason to visit the museum.

There is a privately-run glass shop next door.

Museum of Eastern Bohemia

(Východočeské muzeum)
Eliščino nábřeží 465
CZ-500 34
Hradec Králové
Tel. (049) 234 16
Open Tues.-Sun. 9am-12pm, 1pm-5pm

This regional museum pays tribute to the artistry of the glassmakers of eastern Bohemia in eight display cases featuring predominantly 19th-century colored glass, with an interesting selection of Art Nouveau.

Ethnographic Museum

(Národopisné museum)
CZ-468 22 Horní Pojizeří
v Železném Brodě
Tel. (0428) 722 54, 721 37
Open May-Sept., daily 8:30am-12pm, 1pm-4pm, Oct.-April, Sun. till 12pm, 1pm-4pm

Here you can see what a typical 19th-century bead-maker's workshop looked like, as well as numerous examples of glass manufactured in Železný Brod (Eisenbrod) down through the centuries. Among the exhibits are glass bracelets once exported in vast quantities to India, where they were ritually thrown into the Ganges. The flower wreaths woven from multiple strands of tiny glass "seed beads" framed on the wall should not be missed: in the last century they were placed on the graves of loved ones in a custom peculiar to the Železný Brod area.

The museum is housed in the only log building still standing on the main square - a reminder of a time when the whole town was built of wood.

Harrachov Glass Museum
(Sklářské museum)
Nový Svět 376
CZ-512 46 Harrachov
Tel. (0432) 929 347
Open April-June, Oct.-Dec. 19, Mon.-Fri. 9am-4pm, Sat. till 1pm, July-Sept., Dec. 20-March, Tues.-Sat. till 4pm, Sun. till 1pm.

The development of the *Harrachov* glassworks, one of the oldest and most distinguished in Bohemia, is chronicled in a one-room museum on the main thoroughfare winding through the town, which is a popular winter-sports center. Numerous decorative styles are on display, including some examples of the Art Nouveau glass for which *Harrachov* was famed.

Driving north, turn right at the fork in the road and watch for the wooden sign.

In the same building as the museum but accessible by separate entrance is a shop selling contemporary *Harrachov* glass.

Sázava Castle
Museum of Technical Glass
(Muzeum Technického skla)
Zámek
CZ-285 06 Sázava nad Sázavou
Tel. (0328) 911 77
Open May-Oct., Tues.-Sun. 9am-3pm

This permanent exhibition on the development and uses of industrial glass, in particular that produced at the *Kavalier* factory nearby, will appeal more to the scientifically inclined than to art glass enthusiasts. *Kavalier* specializes in flameproof kitchenware and technical glass.

Exit the Prague-Brno highway at Sázava. The castle is in the center of town.

Lenora Museum
(Muzeum Lenora)
CZ-384 42 Lenora
Tel. (0339) 988 34
Open April-Sept., Tues.-Fri. 9am-3:30pm, by appointment only out of season.

This two-room museum, in the same building as the town hall, features a selection of 19th-century cased glass and Art Nouveau objects produced at the *Lenora* glassworks. Sadly, its most valuable pieces were stolen in a still unsolved 1992 robbery.

There is a shop in the building selling contemporary *Eleonora* glass.

Silesian Museum
(Slezské muzeum)
Sady u muzea 1
CZ-746 01 Opava
Tel. (0653) 21 13 06, Fax 21 53 86
Open Tues.-Fri. 9am-12pm, 1pm-4pm, Sat.-Sun. till 12pm, 1pm-5pm

Only about five percent of the 1,500-piece glass collection is on view, but the periods covered range from medieval to 20th-century. In particular the museum recalls the 18th century, when the glassworks of Silesia rivaled those of neighboring northern Bohemia as producers of engraved glass destined for the aristocratic households of Europe.

Slovak Glass Museum
(Slovenské Sklárske muzeum)
SK-020 61 Lednické Rovne
Tel. (0825) 9338 24, Fax 9338 73

Open Mon.-Fri. 8am-3:30pm

Opened in 1988 in the former mansion of the Schreiber family, founders of the *Lednické Rovne* glassworks, this nicely laid-out collection traces the history of glass manufacturing in Slovakia. Highlights include examples of filigree "pantograph" etching, and turn-of-the-century colored glass from the *Katarínska Huta* works.

Municipal Museum, Exhibition of Decorative Arts

(Mestské muzeum, expozícia
  umeleckých remesiel)
SK-Beblavého 1, Bratislava
Tel. (07) 33 14 73
Open Wed.-Mon. 10am-5pm

Sixty pieces of historical glass from Slovakia are exhibited in this charming little museum, though hundreds more remain in storage due to financial constraints and lack of space.

The museum is in an old quarter on the castle hill.

Šariš Regional Museum

(Šarišské muzeum)
Radnične námestie 13
SK-085 01 Bardejov
Tel. (0935) 6038
Open Tues.-Sun. 9am-12pm,
  12:30pm-6pm

A quarter of the 1,000-piece glass collection is currently on display. The exhibition testifies to the existence, up until this century, of half a dozen glassworks in the Šariš region of eastern Slovakia.

There are also exhibits on local history, folk architecture, icons, and natural history. The museum is on Bardejov's main square, which is lined with medieval houses and also has a Gothic church and town hall.

Museum of Eastern Slovakia in Košice

(Východoslovenské muzeum Košice)
Hviezdoslavova 3
SK-040 01 Košice
Tel. (095) 622 03 09
Open Mon.-Fri. 9am-5pm, Sun. till 1pm

Košice, a large town in eastern Slovakia, was a glassmaking center in the 18th and 19th centuries, but only five of the 50-odd household glass factories that dotted the countryside have survived. The museum, located in the city center, has a permanent exhibition of glass drawn from its 1,500-piece collection; displays change frequently.

Passau Glass Museum

(Glasmuseum Passau)
Hotel Wilder Mann
Am Rathausplatz
D-8390 Passau, Germany
Tel. (0851) 350 71
Open daily 9am-7pm

The biggest collection of Bohemian glass is not in fact in Bohemia, but in the picturesque Danube town of Passau in neighboring Bavaria. With 30,000 pieces, this is also the largest glass museum in Europe. It is family-owned, and half of its holdings, which Georg Höltl began collecting in 1959, are on view in 35 rooms spread out over four floors. Of special interest is the Art Nouveau glass from the *Johann Loetz Witwe* works in Klášterský Mlýn (Klostermühle).

Passau is a three-hour drive southwest of Prague. Head down Rte. 4 via the old glassmaking town of Vimperk. Once in Passau, follow the signs to the city center ("Stadtzentrum"), crossing the first bridge. Turn left onto the embankment. The museum is in the Hotel Wilder Mann next to the town hall.

SCHOOLS

SINCE glassmaking is a trade traditionally passed down from generation to generation, children in many Czech and Slovak communities start out learning about glass at home. Future glassblowers attend a two-to three-year technical school from the age of 14, and then compete for factory apprenticeships.

An aspiring glass designer enters a special glassmaking secondary school at 14. These schools - there are four in the Czech Republic and one in

schools have earned a reputation for excellence beyond the borders of the former Czechoslovakia. Graduates may choose to go on to apply for a coveted place at the Academy of Applied Arts in Prague or the Academy of Fine Arts in Bratislava. There are 25 openings a year at the former and 15 at the latter. The students earn the equivalent of a masters' degree after six years of study.

Almost every Czech and Slovak glass artist of note has graduated from one of the following schools,

The prestigious Prague Academy of Applied Arts. Photograper: Diane Foulds.

Slovakia - offer training in every aspect of glassmaking, and standards are high. Students are given fixed four-year curricula and allowed little time for creative experimentation. The thinking behind this rigidity is that an artist has his or her whole life to develop an individual style, but only a few years to acquire a solid foundation in theory and technique. As a result, the

often spending the final years of the program working in the studio of a well-known artist, such as Libenský or Kopecký. As all these schools are public, tuition for Czechs and Slovaks is free for the time being. Foreigners may study at any of these schools, but must apply well in advance, pay tuition, look long and hard for housing, and be prepared to learn Czech or Slovak.

University-level:

**The Prague Academy
of Applied Arts**
(Vysoká škola umělecko-
průmyslová Praha)
Náměstí Jana Palacha 2
CZ-116 91 Prague 1
Tel. (02) 24 81 11 72

The "UMPRUM," as it is commonly known, is Europe's oldest
college of applied arts. In addition
to offering degrees in ceramics,
textile design, and other subjects,
it has a strong glassmaking
department. No glass-cutting is
taught. The head of the glass
studio is Vladimír Kopecký.
Foreigners can register for the
six-year M.A. program, or take
part in a one-semester exchange.
Write to Mrs. Jiřina Nováková for
information. The deadline for
applications is November 30.

**The Bratislava Academy
of Fine Arts**
(Vysoká škola výtvarných umení
ve Bratislavě)
Hviezdoslavovo námestie 18
SK-814 37 Bratislava
Tel. (07) 33 22 51, Fax 33 23 40

This is the leading art college in
Slovakia. The glass studio, headed
for many years by Václav Cigler
and currently by Juraj Gavula, has
courses in architectural-scale glass
design.
Foreigners can attend a six-
month, two-year, or four-year
course. Write to Mr. Juraj Gavula
or Mr. Ján Mýtny for information.

Secondary Schools:

Secondary School of Glassmaking
(Stredná priemyselná škola sklárská)

SK-020 61 Lednické Rovne,
Slovakia
Tel. (0825) 933 611

Slovakia's only glassmaking school
at the secondary level began its
first academic year in 1993,
teaching design, technical glass,
and glassblowing. Director: Ing.
Ondrej Divinský.

**Železný Brod
Special Glassmaking School**
(Střední uměleckoprůmyslová
škola)
Smetanovo zátiší 470
CZ-468 22 Železný Brod
Tel. (0428) 725 60

A four-year course of study is
offered in seven subjects:
glassblowing, cutting, engraving,
painting, etching, figurines, and
jewelry. The last two subjects are
a specialty of the school. Technical glass is also taught. Established
in 1920. Director: Pavel Ježek.

**Kamenický Šenov
Special Glassmaking School**
(Střední uměleckoprůmyslová
škola)
CZ-471 14 Kamenický Šenov
Tel. (0428) 923 25

The school is believed to be the
oldest of its kind in the world. Its
curriculum is similar to that of the
school in Železný Brod, apart from
figurines and jewelry. Established
in 1856. Director: Karel Rybáček.

**Jablonec nad Nisou
School of Costume Jewelry**
(Střední uměleckoprůmyslová
škola bižuterní)
Horní náměstí 1
CZ-466 01 Jablonec nad Nisou
Tel. (0428) 259 88

The school offers basic glassmaking techniques, but specializes in bead and jewelry production. Established in 1880. Director: Jiří Dostál.

Nový Bor
Special Glassmaking School
(Střední uměleckoprůmyslová
  škola sklářská)

Wolkerova 316
CZ-473 01 Nový Bor
Tel. (0424) 3215

The school offers instruction in glass technology in general, with special attention to glass decoration, a Nový Bor specialty since the 18th century. Established in 1870. Director: Pavel Zatloukal.

ART GALLERIES

Contemporary glass art, or studio glass, is difficult to find in Prague. A number of art galleries hold occasional glass exhibitions, but very few specialize in the field.

Galerie Böhm
Anglická 1
CZ-120 00 Prague 2
Tel./Fax (02) 236 20 16
Open Tues.-Fri. 2pm-6pm, Sat.-Sun. 10am-3pm
Credit cards

This was the first gallery dedicated to contemporary art glass to open in Prague after the 1989 revolution. In the showroom, which is below street level, you'll find works that rank among the best being produced anywhere in the world. The gallery's English-speaking owner, Jiří Böhm, will tell you anything you want to know about the glass art scene.

The gallery entrance is on Legerova street, the three-lane highway behind and to the right of the National Museum at the top of Václavské náměstí (Wenceslas Square). Look for the sign.

Galerie Rob van den Doel
Jánský vršek 15
CZ-118 00 Prague 1
Tel./Fax (02) 533 92 71
Open daily 10:30am-5pm
Traveler's checks, credit cards

Rob van den Doel is a Dutch glass collector whose main gallery is in The Hague. This gallery in Prague features the work of leading Czech and Slovak glass artists, as well as artists from other countries, in particular Hungary and Poland. If you're walking along Nerudova ulice towards Prague Castle, the shop is about two-thirds of the way up, on a street with narrow stairs running off to the left.

Genia Loci
Újezd 11
CZ-150 00 Prague 5
Tel. / Fax (02) 53 94 68
Open Mon.-Fri. 10am-6pm.

While not devoted specifically to art glass, this new gallery often exhibits it along with other types of contemporary design. Located on Újezd, not far from the funicular boarding station.

ARTISTS

There are currently about 180 recognized glass artists working in the Czech and Slovak Republics. The following is a list of the best known. Most have works in the decorative arts museums of the world's major capitals, as well as in such important collections as the Corning Museum of Glass in Corning, N.Y., and London's Victoria and Albert Museum. Ironically, there are few places to see these artists' work in Prague or Bratislava, apart from the handful of galleries on page 153.

The 22 artists listed here are only the tip of the iceberg. Not included are some of the numerous stars who have emerged from the studios of Stanislav Libenský and Václav Cigler, such as Anna Kopecká, Pavel Trnka, Ivana Houserová, Juraj Opršal, František Janák, Milan Handl, Zdeněk Lhotský, Ivo Rozsypal, Jaroslav Róna, Jiří Nekovář, Eliška Rožátová, Gizela Šabóková, and Aleš Vašíček. These artists differ from one another so radically in style and approach that their work soon becomes easy to recognize.

For more information about Czech and Slovak glass artists, contact Galerie Böhm, Galerie Rob van den Doel, or the Glass Association (see "Art Galleries" and "Associations" in Part Six).

"Untitled-vase", František Vízner, 1987. Cut glass with matte finish, 22 cm. Photographer: Gabriel Urbánek.

Jan Exnar's studio, Havlíčkův Brod.
Photographers: Zdenka Kalabisová and
Antonín Krčmář.

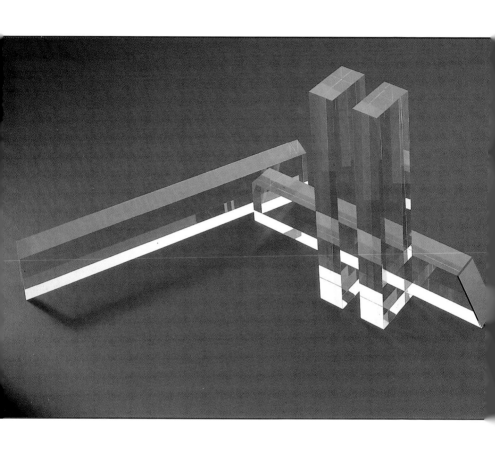

"Untitled," 1992. Cut optical glass,
60 x 110 x 50 cm. Photographer:
Miroslav Vojtěchovský.

VÁCLAV CIGLER
born 1929

The influential Czech glass artist Václav Cigler developed an interest in the optical properties of glass while studying under Josef Kaplický at the Prague Academy of Applied Arts in the 1950s. He enjoyed the way glass reflects, deforms, enhances, and illuminates the objects around it. In the early sixties he started working with huge transparent blocks, making prismatic forms or walls with concave and convex sides. Cigler's chief concern was not the sculpture itself but rather the way it interacted with its environment.

In 1965-79 he promoted new ideas for household glass, jewelry, and glass in architecture as head of the glass studio of the Bratislava Academy of Fine Arts. Now recognized as a pioneer in prismatic sculpture, for decades he has been an important reference point for glass artists, in particular Marian Karel, Oldřich Plíva, Yan Zoritchak, Aleš Vašíček, and Pavel Trnka. A Cigler sculpture from 1985 can be seen in the upper hall of Prague's Náměstí Republiky metro station: six columns of laminated glass gleam in different hues depending on the angle from which they are viewed.

BOHUMIL ELIÁŠ
born 1937

Spontaneous and free-spirited would be the best way to describe the work of Bohumil Eliáš. Frequently he combines glass with another medium, such as oil on canvas, or burns colored powder into a glass shape while it is still hot. The result is richly abstract, with streaks of color that reflect his classical training in painting, drawing, and sculpture. Eliáš studied glassmaking in Železný Brod and spent the early 1960s in the glass studio of Josef Kaplický at the Academy of Applied Arts. He created a five-meter glass water fountain that drew raves at Expo '67 in Montreal and was ultimately purchased by the Canadian government. In the 1970s, the Shah of Iran commissioned him to design stained-glass windows for a number of 13th-century mosques. Unfortunately, few survived the Islamic Revolution of 1979. Eliáš's work is scattered throughout the Czech Republic, often in unlikely places (he designed a glass wall mosaic on the exterior of a bank in Vimperk, for example). His work is also found in Paris, Amsterdam, Yokohama, and in many German cities.

"Microworld", 1991. Cut, fused, and painted glass, 13 x 13 x 13 cm.
Photographer: Gabriel Urbánek.

JAN EXNAR
born 1951

Jan Exnar designs painted
window panels set in lead. What
is striking about his work is the
raw, expressive quality of the
painting. The lead partitions act as
part of the design, and the artist
may insert a slice of colored glass,
or apply other techniques such as
sandblasting or etching. When
Exnar sculpts in glass, he usually
focuses on a single color or a
basic shape, such as a simple
curved cylinder, globe, or rec-
tangle. One of his earlier pieces is
a glass likeness of a rumpled
pillow.

Exnar attended the Special
Glassmaking School in Železný
Brod in the latter half of the
1960s, and studied under
Stanislav Libenský at the Prague
Academy of Applied Arts.
Some of his experimental work
has been produced at the *Beránek*
glassworks in Škrdlovice.

Painted and cut window panel,
110 x 110 cm. Photographer:
Gabriel Urbánek.

JAN FIŠAR
born 1933

Motion is a source of inspiration for Jan Fišar, whose highly abstract work evokes the qualities of metal or plastic. Fišar in fact often combines metal into his pieces, which sometimes take the form of casually shaped reliefs applied to architecture or lighting fixtures. Much of Fišar's work looks like something in the process of opening, unrolling, or freezing in mid-air, even when it represents a thoroughly prosaic subject, as in the case of his *Cat and Dog*, or

Life and Death of a Bachelor. A Fišar piece is generally opaque and glossy, anything but geometric, and made of remelted and reground glass.

Fišar studied from 1953-59 under Josef Wagner, a leading Czech sculptor, at the Prague Academy of Applied Arts. He worked in stone and wood before turning to glass, and spent the early part of his glassmaking career at the *Železný Brod* works.

"Dancing Couple," remelted glass Photographers Zdenka Kalabisová an‹ Antonín Krčm‹

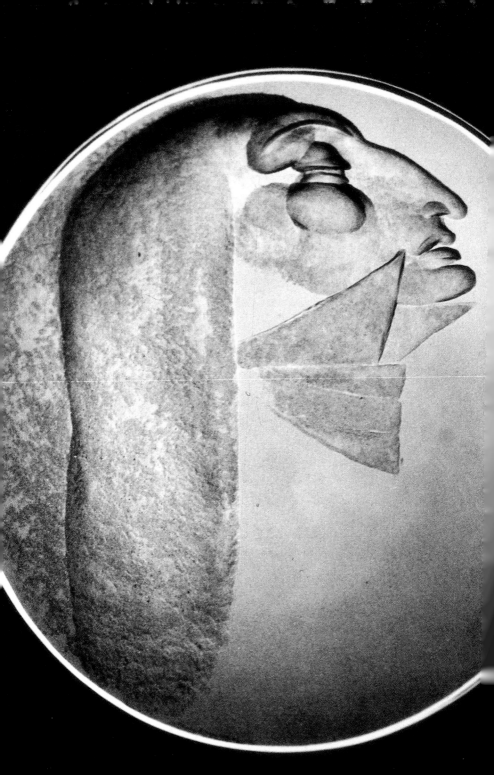

JIŘÍ HARCUBA
born 1928

"Paganini," 1984.
Engraved glass,
15 cm.
Photographer:
Jindřich Brok.

Jiří Harcuba is a master of portrait engraving. He uses the shadows and light inherent in glass to give a portrait its sculptural surfaces. Harcuba's artistry finds expression on plaques, medals, coins, and sculpture. His portraits may be moving, pensive, or humorous, but what they all aim to do is capture the psyche and personality of the subject, whether it be Mahatma Gandhi or Albert Einstein. Harcuba also makes bronze medals. He learned engraving in Harrachov, where he was born, and later studied in Nový Bor. Bohemian portrait engraving - a tradition that goes back to the early 17th century - attracted the interest of many Czechoslovak artists up until the 1960s. But it has virtually died out since then, and Harcuba is the last outstanding glass portrait engraver left in Central Europe.

Harcuba taught at the Royal College of Art in London in 1965-66, and since 1983 he has taught engraving at schools in California, New York, Washington, D.C., and elsewhere. He was head of the Prague Academy of Applied Arts from 1990 to 1994.

PAVEL HLAVA
born 1924

Pavel Hlava's work has developed over the years from purely functional glassware designs to abstract art forms that have won numerous international awards. In the 1940s and 1950s he concentrated on engraving; in the 1960s and 1970s he turned to modern colored vase forms and finally, in the 1980s, to cut glass. His focus now is on studio glass, into which he synthesizes all his previous experimentation. His artistic output is highly varied, but characteristically it is brightly colored and geometrical.

Hlava started his training at the secondary school for glassmaking in Železný Brod, and studied at the Prague Academy of Applied Arts under Karel Štipl. At *Crystalex*, where he was chief designer for almost 20 years, some of the most popular handblown and mass-produced drinking sets were produced from his designs. Hlava is one of the most widely exhibited Czech glass artists, with pieces in museum collections all over the world.

"Energy," 1986. Cut and fused glass, 60 x 30 cm. Photographer: Miroslav Vojtěchovský.

MARIAN KAREL
born 1944

There is a monumental feel to everything Marian Karel produces, whether it be small block-like shapes or wall-sized forms. Karel takes massive blocks of glass and models out simple architectural shapes that exude an air of strength. A student of Stanislav Libenský at the Prague Academy of Applied Arts, he spent the 1980s creating large architectural compositions of glass panels either fused together or connected with metal braces. One of his larger pieces is at the entrance to the Finnish Glass Museum in Riihimäki.

Karel, who attended the secondary school of glass and jewelry in Jablonec nad Nisou, currently teaches at the glass studio of the Prague Academy of Applied Arts. His work is in Corning, N.Y., Budapest, Moscow, Tokyo, Kyoto, Paris, and in many cities in Germany.

"Ruby towers", 198C
Mould-melted glass,
30 cm. Photographe
Gabriel Urbánek.

170

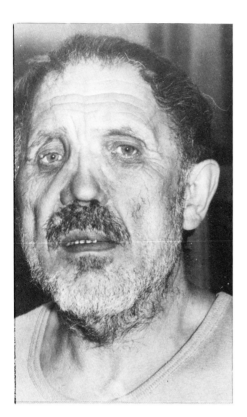

VLADIMÍR KOPECKÝ
born 1931

Vladimír Kopecký's work often takes the form of sandblasted or painted sheets of glass stacked or arranged together in abstract compositions. Sometimes they have a three-dimensional character and combine glass with other materials, such as wood or metal, making his works a mixed-media affair. Kopecký is regarded by many as a painter no less than as a glass artist, since he often works in oil on canvas, using a jumble of bright colors. Kopecký began his training after World War II in the glassmaking schools at Kamenický Šenov and Nový Bor. Josef Kaplický was his teacher at the Prague Academy of Applied Arts. After 1950, he worked regularly with architects, designing panels and wall mosaics. Kopecký has had a major impact on younger generations of Czech and Slovak glass artists. He was appointed director of the glass studio at the Prague Academy of Applied Arts in 1990.

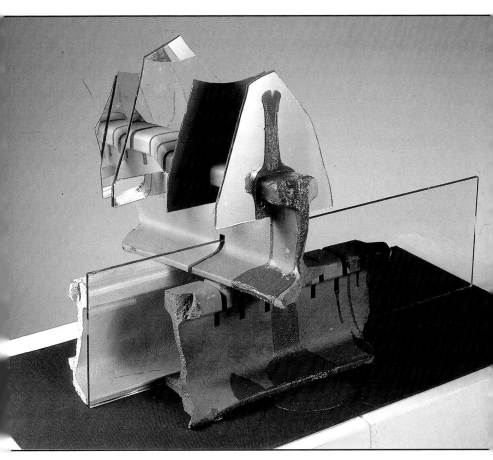

"Blind Track," 1987. Painted glass,
46 x 50 x 50 cm. Photographer:
Miroslav Vojtěchovský.

STANISLAV LIBENSKÝ
born 1922

& JAROSLAVA BRYCHTOVÁ
born 1924

Stanislav Libenský and Jaroslava Brychtová rank among the world's greatest living glass sculptors, and they are still at the peak of their creativity. The work of this husband-and-wife team - characterized by simple block shapes that seem to draw in light and infuse the mass with color and nuance - cannot be mistaken for that of anyone else. Working in their rooftop studio on Wenceslas Square, Libenský and Brychtová have created monumental sculptures that have strongly influenced the international studio glass movement. Several commissions have come from the Corning Museum of Glass in Corning, N.Y. Their work is also represented in London's Victoria and Albert Museum, the Metropolitan Museum of Art in New York, the Musée des Arts Decoratifs in Paris, the Sydney Museum of Applied Arts and Sciences, and Tokyo's National Museum of Modern Art. Sculptures by the couple also grace the headquarters of the United Nations in New York and of UNESCO in Paris.

The couple met in the 1950s at the glassmaking secondary school in Železný Brod, and have been working together ever since. They sketch an idea and model it into a three-dimensional shape, and with the help of glassmakers at the Železný Brod works, the idea metamorphoses into glass, a process that usually takes from two weeks to a month. Libenský headed the glass studio of Prague's Academy of Applied Arts from 1963-87, inspiring two generations of glass artists.

Some of their past work can be seen just by strolling around Prague. They designed the glass-sheathed exterior of the Nová Scéna annex next to the National Theater opera house on Národní třída, and new windows for the St. Wenceslas chapel in St. Vitus cathedral. They have sculptures in the main hall of the former federal parlament building; in the wedding hall of the Old Town Hall; in the reception area of the Hotel Atrium; and in the Palace of Culture, built in the 1980s.

"Diagonal," 1989. Mould-melted glass, 80 x 60 x 25 cm. Photographers: Zdenka Kalabisová and Antonín Krčmář.

MICHAL MACHAT
born 1963

MARTIN VELÍŠEK
born 1963

Windows for St. Wenceslas chapel, St. Vitus cathedral, 1964-69. Mould-melted glass, 700 x 120 cm. Photographers: Zdenka Kalabisová and Antonín Krčmář.

Michal Machat and Martin Velíšek are the *enfants terribles* of the contemporary Czech art glass scene. Their vases, sculptures, and windows are bold to the point of brutality. Nearly the entire surface of the glass is covered with paint, and the subject matter is intended to shock: skeletons, nudity, genitals, stabbings, desolate apartment scenes.

Both artists studied at the Prague Academy of Applied Arts under Stanislav Libenský and his successor, Jaroslav Svoboda, and often exhibit together. While Velíšek's painting owes something to primitive art, Machat's work is more stylized, with his earlier vases faintly reminiscent of Egyptian hieroglyphics. Only on the scene since the late 1980s, both Machat and Velíšek are collecting a growing number of fans in international circles.

"Helmutek" by Michal Machat, 1990. Painted glass panel. Photographers: Zdenka Kalabisová and Antonín Krčmář.

"Swimming Pool" by Martin Velíšek, 1991. Hot-shaped and painted glass. Photographer: Gabriel Urbánek.

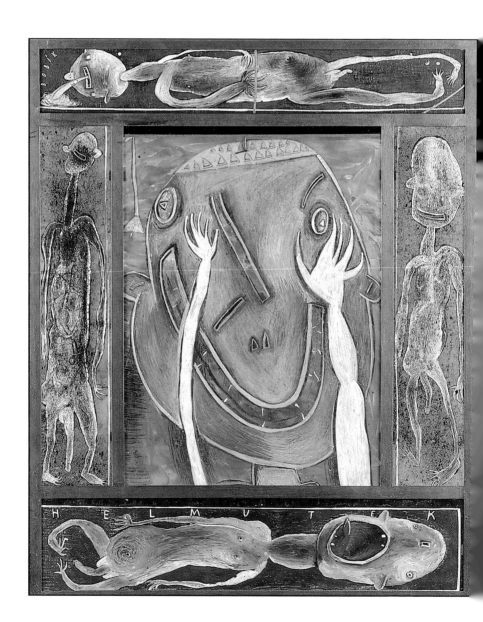

IVANA MAŠITOVÁ
born 1961

As in the case of so many of her contemporaries, Ivana Mašitová's unique talent lies in her painting, although she has also produced mould-melted glass sculptures and window panels. She is best known for a series of boxes and vases naturalistically painted in black, gold, or earth tones; there is an organic quality to her patterns evoking Asian or African art. Mašitová also cuts, engraves, and sandblasts glass. Many of her pieces are vases, boxes, or bowls that are utilitarian as well as beautiful to look at.

Mašitová attended the special glassmaking school in Kamenický Šenov, and studied under Stanislav Libenský and Jaroslav Svoboda at the Prague Academy of Applied Arts.

Vase, 1988. Painted glass, height 25cm. Photographer: Gabriel Urbánek.

JAROSLAV MATOUŠ
born 1941

Jaroslav Matouš aims for things other glass artists try to avoid: cracks, chips, fissures, and jutting edges. The classic Matouš piece is a cylinder of paper-thin glass that is cut, painted, and decorated with strands of loose wire as well as engraving, laminating, and other touches. He has also produced several large-scale sculptures in architectural settings.

The artist learned to cut, paint, and sandblast glass while a student at the glassmaking secondary school in Železný Brod, but always returned to his favorite decorative method: drawing on glass. A student in Stanislav Libenský's studio from 1961-67, Matouš also studied industrial design for a year and did a stint as a designer for *Moser* in Karlovy Vary. Although his work almost always takes the form of discs or cylinders, Matouš thinks of himself as a painter. "Glass," he says, "is my canvas."

"Morning," 1991. Blown, painted, and carved glass and metal wire, 40 x 30 cm. Photographer: Gabriel Urbánek.

RENÉ ROUBÍČEK
born 1922

René Roubíček has created unique sculptures with his wife, Miluše Roubíčková, since the 1940s, but unlike the Libenský-Brychtová team, the couple have repeatedly gone their separate ways stylistically. Roubíček prefers clear crystal forms, colorful abstractions, and large-scale sculptures, and has also experimented with water fountains, chandeliers, and illuminating sculptures. The glass light fixtures in Prague's Inter-Continental Hotel are his work (1973). He and Roubíčková worked together on a series of heads from the mid-1970s to the early 1980s, then parted ways again.

Roubíček trained at the Prague Academy of Applied Arts in the first half of the 1940s under Josef Holeček, finishing his studies in the early 1950s under Josef Kaplický. He moved to northern Bohemia after the war and taught for seven years at the glassmaking secondary school in Kamenický Šenov. More recently, he has designed glassware for *Egermann-Exbor*. His award-winning work is on display at Prague's National Gallery and in museums in Corning, N.Y., Amsterdam, London, Zürich, and several German cities.

ject" 1991. Blown and sheet glass,
 cm. Photographer:
riel Urbánek.

"Compote jar," 1982. Blown and
hot-shaped glass, 16 x 13cm.
Photographer: Miroslav Vojtěchovský.

MILUŠE ROUBÍČKOVÁ
born 1922

Miluše Roubíčková takes an
everyday object, like a bouquet
of flowers, and turns it into a
playful glass fantasy. Her colorful
work is usually representational.
She might do a platter with glass
fish, a jar of preserves, a red
cake in the shape of a springform,
or a bowl of curiously-colored
fruit.

Like her husband, René,
Roubíčková started out at the
Prague Academy of Applied Arts,
where she studied under Josef
Holeček and Josef Kaplický. Her
early pieces were lead crystal
fruit bowls and stemware sets, as
well as hot-shaped pieces made at
the glassworks in Nový Bor and
Škrdlovice. In later years her work
was influenced by pop art.
Everything coming out of
Roubíčková's studio is unique
on the Czech glass scene. Her
work is in numerous museum
collections throughout the
world, including Corning, N.Y.,
Düsseldorf, Coburg, and
Bombay.

JAROMÍR RYBÁK
born 1951

Jaromír Rybák's glass pieces defy generalization. They may be clear glass forms, window panels with geometric motifs, or colored glass sculptures evoking animals, clouds, trees, or rain. Among the most interesting aspects of his work is the way he combines various colors in a single piece, sometimes irradiating one shade gradually into another. He also works in acrylics and designs for architectural settings, occasionally with fellow artist Gizela Šabóková.

After graduating from the glassmaking secondary school in Železný Brod, Rybák studied under Stanislav Libenský at the Prague Academy of Applied Arts.

"Top of the Sky," 1990. Mould-melted glass, 35 x 50 x 15 cm. Photograph: Zdenka Kalabisová and Antonín Krčmář.

IVANA ŠRÁMKOVÁ-ŠOLCOVÁ
born 1960

Šrámková-Šolcová's work, perhaps more than that of any other Czech or Slovak artist of her generation, is about humor. She rarely produces anything purely abstract, and her intent is to have fun. Her sculptures include a still-life bowl of fruit, a series of automobiles painted in bright, child-like colors, a lady with bright red lipstick, dogs, animals, and a bowl in the shape of a boat. She does hot-shaped glass, molten sculptures, and painted vases. Occasionally she takes on more serious challenges. In a recent project, she designed 12 windows for the 19th-century Anglican church in the spa town of Mariánské Lázně.

The artist studied in Železný Brod and at the Prague Academy of Applied Arts under Stanislav Libenský.

"Me with Honza," 1989. Mould-melted glass, 35 x 50 cm. Photographer: Gabriel Urbánek.

JIŘÍ ŠUHÁJEK
born 1943

Jiří Šuhájek, who has designed for
Moser and *Crystalex*, blows much
of his glassware himself. His
recent sculptures include stylized
birds and abstract shapes, but he
is probably best known for his
subtly erotic human figures, some
of which measure up to 8 feet in
height. What is remarkable about
these shapes is the way they
evoke feminine contours,
especially the long, transparent
legs. They also suggest fragility,
and are ultimately an homage to
Eve.

Šuhájek is virtually the only
contemporary artist who even
attempts to portray the entire
human figure in the medium of
glass.

He was a student of Stanislav
Libenský at the Prague Academy
of Applied Arts and also attended
London's Royal College of Art.
His work can be found in the
Corning Museum of Glass in
Corning, N.Y., the Victoria
and Albert Museum in London,
and many other collections.

Female figure. Blown and hot-shaped
glass. Photographer: Jan Kříž.

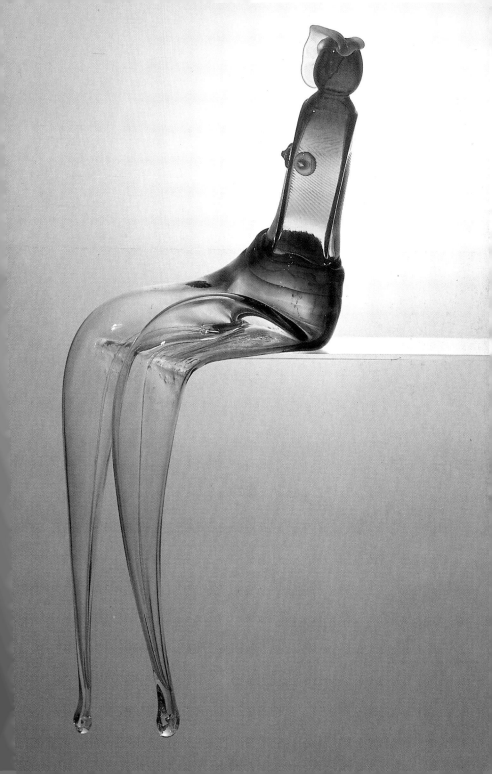

"Bowl," 1987. Red cut glass, 30 cm.
Photographer: Jan Černo.

194

FRANTIŠEK VÍZNER
born 1936

The characteristic František
Vízner piece is a simple, almost
minimalist shape, usually round,
oblong, or flat. It is matte on the
surface and might look functional,
but the impression is deceiving.
The specialness lies in the subtlety
of color - usually only one - and
the way the form diffuses light.
Vízner trained as an apprentice
in Nový Bor, attended the
glassmaking secondary school in
Železný Brod, and graduated
from the Prague Academy of
Applied Arts in 1962, where he
studied under Karel Štipl. He
worked at the former *Beránek*
glassworks in Škrdlovice from
1967-75.

Vízner's sculptures are found in
museum collections in Corning,
N.Y., London, Paris, Zürich,
Lausanne, Düsseldorf, Stockholm,
Tokyo, and Sydney. But none has
been viewed by as large a
segment of the public as the glass
wall castings he designed for
Prague's Karlovo náměstí metro
station.

ASKOLD ŽÁČKO
born 1946

Askold Žáčko is the most famous of Slovakia's glass artists. After attending the secondary glassmaking school in Železný Brod, he enrolled in the Academy of Fine Arts in Bratislava, working in the "Glass in Architecture" studio of Václav Cigler. He replaced Cigler as head of the glass studio in 1979, where he taught until 1990. In many ways influenced by Cigler, Žáčko has produced beautifully geometric, finely modeled pieces with smooth, almost mirror-like surfaces and multiple fused facets. Some of his pieces resemble a glass labyrinth, with layers of mirrors that play optical tricks on the viewer.

Since the mid-eighties, Žáčko has also designed for the *Lednické Rovne* glassworks. At the end of the decade he switched gears and began producing far more abstract, expressive pieces, often in bright colors. Like Cigler, Žáčko has had an immense influence on a whole generation of Slovak glass artists.

"Cave," 1992. Melted, cut, and fused composition glass, 55 x 27 x 17 cm. Photographer: Anna Žáčková.

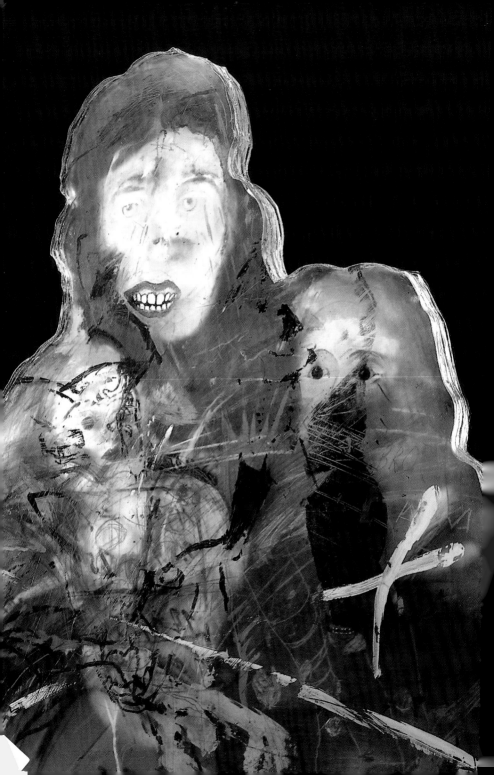

DANA ZÁMEČNÍKOVÁ
born 1945

Dana Zámečníková layers sheets of flat glass, held together on a metal frame, and paints the surfaces with impressions of people, figures, or activity, often street scenes or crowds. The compositions impart a feeling of movement and a delicate mixture of moods and emotions.

Trained as an architect at the Technical University in Prague from 1962-68, she moved on to study theater design under Josef Svoboda at the Prague Academy of Applied Arts. She began her artistic career by experimenting with mobiles, toys, animated designs, and scene painting.

Since 1978, Zámečníková has devoted herself to glass, exhibiting her work around the world. Her pieces are in museum collections in numerous countries, including Germany, Japan, Australia, Britain, France, Switzerland, and the United States.

"Old Photographs," 1991. Painted flat glass. Photographer: Gabriel Urbánek.

ASSOCIATIONS

The Czech Glass Society
(Česká sklářská společnost)
Ševčíkova 9
CZ-130 00 Prague 3
Tel. (02) 27 81 10
For glass experts and other professionals in the field. Founded in 1990 as the Czechoslovak Glass Society. Membership: 3,000. Meets monthly. Holds conferences and lectures on issues relating to the glass industry.

The Silicate Society
(Silikátová Společnost)
Novotného lávka 5
CZ-110 01 Prague 1
Tel. (02) 231 01 24, ext. 337

Acts as a forum for professionals in the glass, ceramics, and construction material industries. Founded in 1923. Membership: 5,000. Meets roughly four times a year. Organizes conferences and promotes commercial contacts. Issues a quarterly magazine, *Silikátový Zpravodaj* (Silicate News).

The Glass Association
(Sklářské sdružení Praha)
Mánes Building
Masarykovo nábřeží 250
CZ-110 00 Prague 1
Tel./Fax (02) 29 38 29
Founded in January 1990 as a forum for glass artists. Membership: 100. Meets irregularly. Holds lectures and exhibitions of modern glass art.

The Association of Czech Glass and Ceramics Producers
(Asociace sklářského a keramického průmyslu ČR)
Mikulandská 7
CZ-113 61 Prague 1
Tel. (02) 29 92 51, Fax 29 78 96

An organization for managers of glass and ceramics factories. Membership: 54. Meets two to three times a year.

SVÚS - The State Research Institute of Glass
(Státní výzkumný ústav sklářský - SVÚS)
Škroupova 957
CZ-501 92 Hradec Králové
Tel. (049) 67 31 11, Fax 61 66 63
Formerly a state research center, now a state-owned joint-stock company. Founded in 1923. Staff: 100. Provides technical and scientific research and development in the field of glass, as well as consulting services in English, French, and German. Library. Publishes a monthly technical magazine, *Sklář a Keramik* (Glassmaker and Potter), in Czech with English, German, and French summaries.

The Association of Costume Jewelry Manufacturers
(Svaz výrobců bižuterie)
Podhorská 54
CZ-466 01 Jablonec nad Nisou
Tel. (0428) 226 55, Fax 229 47
Acts as a forum for large and small, primarily private costume jewelry enterprises in the Jablonec nad Nisou area. Membership: 24.

The Branch Union of the [Slovak] Glass and Costume Jewelry Industry
(Odvetvový zväz sklárskeho a bižutérneho priemyslu)
Drieňová 24
SK-826 03 Bratislava
Tel. (0427) 23 34 31, Fax 23 35 42
A trade union for the Slovak glass and glass costume jewelry industries. Membership: 13 Slovak glass enterprises.

The Guild of Private Manufacturers of Jablonec Goods
(Cech soukromých výrobců
jabloneckého zboží)
Za plynárnou 1
CZ-466 01 Jablonec nad Nisou

Tel./Fax (0428) 295 17
Founded in 1991 to protect the interests of private manufacturers of household glass, glass giftware, and glass costume jewelry. Membership: 56. Meets monthly.

GLASS VOCABULARY

The following is a brief glossary of glass terms in Czech, Slovak, and English.

English	Czech	Slovak
ashtray	popelník	popolník
antique	starožitnost	starožitnosť
beads	korálky	korálky
blown glass	foukané sklo	fúkané sklo
bottle	láhev	fľaša
bowl	mísa	misa
bowl (of a glass)	mísa	misa
bubble	bublinka	bublinka
button	knoflík	gombík
cast glass	lité sklo	liate sklo
champagne glass	šampaňka	pohár na šampanské
candlestick	svícen	svietnik
carafe	karafa	karafa
carved	řezané	rezané
chandelier	lustr	luster
colored glass	barevné sklo	farebné sklo
cup	číše	čaša
(sundae) cup	pohár	pohár
cut glass	broušené sklo	brúsené sklo
crystal	křišťál	krišťáľ
decanter	láhev	fľaša
decoration	zdobení	dekorovanie
dish	talíř	tanier
drinking set	nápojový soubor	nápojová sada
engraved glass	ryté sklo	ryté sklo
etched	leptané	leptané
export permit	povolení k vývozu	povolenie k vývozu
flaw	chyba	chyba
flute	flétna	flauta
foot	dýnko	dienko
gilded	pozlacené	pozlátené
glass	sklo	sklo
glazed	glazurované	glazované
a glass	sklenice	pohár
goblet	kalich	kalich
handmade	ruční práce	ručná práca
high enamel	vysoký smalt	vysoký smalt
hot-shaped glass	hutně tvarované	hutne tvarované
insurance	pojištění	poistenie
iridized	irizované	irizovanie
jardiniere	žardiniera	žardiniera
jewelry	bižuterie	bižutéria

lead	olovo	olovo
lead crystal	olovnatý křišťál	olovnatý krištáľ
machine-made	strojní výroba	strojová výroba
melted glass	tavené sklo	tavené sklo
mug	džbánek	džbánik
necklace	náhrdelník	náhrdelník
overlay glass	přejímané sklo	prejímané sklo
painted glass	malované sklo	maľované sklo
paneled glass	lištovačka	lištovačka
paperweight	těžítko	ťažítko
pitcher	džbán	džbán
plate	talíř	tanier
plate glass	ploché sklo	ploché sklo
polished	leštěné	leštené
pressed glass	lisované sklo	lisované sklo
punch bowl	bowle	bowle
glass raw base	sklovina	sklovina
receipt	paragon	paragon
sandblasted	pískované	pieskované
sculpture	socha/plastika	socha/plastika
sheet glass	tabulové sklo	tabuľové sklo
stained-glass window	vitráž/vitrail	vitráž/vitraj
stem	nožka	nôžka
stopper	zátka	zátka
studio glass	ateliérové sklo	ateliérové sklo
tumbler	odlievka	odlievka
tray	podnos	podnos
vase	váza	váza
window panel	okenní vitráž	okenná vitráž

GLOSSARY:

Cased or layered glass - glass is covered with a layer of transparent colored glass, then designs are cut through the surface to expose the clear glass underneath. Usually done on lead crystal.

Enameled glass - a transparent painted design fired so that the enamel looks like transparent colored glass.

Etched glass - glass is covered with an acid-resistant layer such as wax, oil, or varnish, and a design is scratched on the surface with a needle. It is then dipped in a bath of hydrofluoric acid, which etches the scratched surfaces indelibly.

Forest glass - a greenish glass made in the Middle Ages from potash made from the ashes of burned trees.

Gold-sandwich glass - a gold design is fixed between two fused layers of glass. Also known by the German term, *Zwischengoldglas.*

Hot-shaped glass - glass that is shaped into its final form while still in its molten state, without the use of moulds. Also called "off-hand shaped" glass.

High enamel - a highly ornate decorating style on colored glass. Broad surfaces are painted with gold leaf, which is decorated with a relief of opaque flowers made of a glass-ceramic paste.

Hyalite glass - an opaque colored glass, usually black or red, looking something like sealing wax. Sometimes painted with gold chinoiserie designs.

Iridized glass - made popular in the Art Nouveau period; having an iridescent surface by the application of a thin metallic film, such as tin chloride and barium nitrate.

Jade glass - a bright green opaque glass, usually used for vases, urns, ashtrays, or animal figurines, such as turtles. Also called malachite glass.

Lithyaline glass - a marble-like glass finish resembling semi-precious stone, produced in numerous colors, made popular by Friedrich Egermann in the 1830s.

Opal glass - white or pastel-colored glass that is partly translucent.

Overlay glass - glass is covered with a layer of transparent colored glass, then a third layer of white enamel, through which designs are cut, exposing the colored and clear glass underneath. The white enamel surface is usually painted with flowers and gilded for added effect.

Milk glass - an opaque white glass, popularized in the first half of the 19th century in northern Bohemia, whose aim was to resemble porcelain. Often painted with rose motifs.

Paneled glass - a decorating style in which transparent glass is cased with colored glass "panels" finished with tiny gilded leaves and decoration. Also known as "lištovačka", or leaf design.

Sandblasting - an engraving method involving the blowing of sharp-grained sand onto the glass surface to achieve a decorative frosted pattern.

Stained glass - glass painted with a metallic coating and then fired in a furnace. A silver coating produces a yellow stain, and a copper coating produces black when fired twice, red when fired three times. Made famous by Friedrich Egermann in the 19th century.

Uranium glass - a glaze made from uranium oxide that produced a fluorescent lime or yellow color. Developed about 1840 by the *Riedel* glassworks in Polubný (today part of *Desná*).

BIBLIOGRAPHY

Baldwin, Gary and Carno, Lee, *Moser - Artistry in Glass 1857-1938,* Antique Publications: Marietta, Ohio, 1988.

The Corning Museum of Glass, *Czechoslovakian Glass 1350-1980,* Dover Publications: New York, 1981.

Czechoslovak Glass Review/ Glass Review/New Glass Review (Prague, 1985-93).

Drahotová, Olga, *Evropské sklo,* Artia: Prague, 1985.

Durdík, Jan, *The Pictorial Encyclopedia of Antiques,* Hamlyn: London, 1970.

Heacock, William, "Czech Glass," in *Collecting Glass,* vol. II, Richardson Printing Corporation: Marietta, Ohio, 1985.

Hetteš, Karel, *Glass in Czechoslovakia,* SNTL: Prague, 1958.

Hetteš, Karel, "Die Glaserzeugung in der Slowakei: Geschichte einer tausendjährigen Entwicklung, I-IV," *Czechoslovak Glass Review* (1974), vol. XXIX, nos. 8-12.

Kaba, Arnošt, *Sklářství na Vysočině,* exhibition catalogue, Muzeum Vysočiny v Jihlavě: Jihlava, 1972.

Langhamer, Antonín, and Pekař,

Ladislav, *Bohemia Crystal, Sklo které dobylo svět,* Skloexport a.s.: Liberec, 1991.

Maternová, Věra, "The History of the Manufacture of Glass Stones and Costume Jewelry in Bohemia," in *Jewels of Fantasy: Costume Jewelry of the 20th Century,* catalogue, Swarovski Company: 1992.

Moravská galerie v Brně, *Český porcelán a sklo 19. století,* Brno, 1992.

Museum of Glass and Costume Jewelry, Jablonec nad Nisou, *Riedel Since 1756, 10 Generations of Glassmakers,* exhibition catalogue, 1991.

Passauer Glasmuseum, *Böhmisches Glas, Phänomen europäischer Kultur 1700-1950,* museum guide, Passau, 1993.

Petrová, Sylva, Drahotová, Olga, ed., Musée des Arts Decoratifs, *Verres de Bohême,* Flammarion: Paris, 1989.

Prague Glass Prize '91, catalogue of an exhibition organized at the Mánes exhibition hall, Prague, by the Union of Creative Artists, the Glass Association, and the Heller Gallery, New York, Aug. 22-Sept. 22, 1991.

Vondruška, V., and Langhamer, A., *Bohemian Glass, Tradition and Present,* Crystalex: Nový Bor, 1991.